CONC.

CONCILIUM 2001/4

IN SEARCH OF UNIVERSAL VALUES

Edited by

Karl-Josef Kuschel and Dietmar Mieth

SCM Press · London

Published by SCM Press, 9–17 St Albans Place, London N1

ISBN: 0 334 03065 X

Printed by Biddles Ltd, Guildford and King's Lynn

Concilium Published February, April, June, October,
December

Contents

III. Applications

Documentation

Introduction: In Search of Universal Values

KARL–JOSEF KUSCHEL AND DIETMAR MIETH

The complexity of the world situation, which has been intensified by the globalization of the markets, has sparked off a lively inter-cultural discussion about the possibility and urgency of universally valid moral values, norms and rules which are recognized by all peoples and states, cultures and religions. More markedly than ever, the representatives of the world religions are confronted with expectations that they should utilize the resources of spirituality and wisdom to further peace and justice world-wide. The Peace Summit of Religious Leaders to be held in New York in September 2001, to which the General Secretary of the United Nations, Kofi Anan, has issued invitations, is impressive evidence of these expectations.

In this issue of *Concilium* we want to make a contribution to such discussions of universal values. We begin in Part I by documenting how they are reflected in churches and movements. Thus in an address to the Papal Academy of Social Sciences on 27 April 2001 the present pope, John Paul II, argued for a common ethical code for humankind. Here he was guided by the conviction that the norms of social life must be sought in human beings themselves, in universal humanity as it emerged from the hand of the Creator. Such a quest is unavoidable if globalization is not just to be another name for the absolute relativizing of values and the homogenization of lifestyles and cultures. We have included the text here in full.

We have similarly included a noteworthy statement by the World Council of Churches at its Eighth General Assembly in Harare in 1998. In his report, the President, Katholikos Aram I, called for the development of a fundamental shared ethic. For such an ethic he referred to the 1993 Declaration of the Parliament of the World's Religions. We have quoted the most important passages from this report. We are particularly grateful to the present General Secretary of the World Council of Churches, Dr Konrad Raiser, for being ready to expand his contribution on the theme of 'Global Order and Global Ethic' in the light of the most recent developments at very short notice and making his contribution available to *Concilium*.

As is well known, the 1993 Parliament of the World's Religions issued a first programmatic declaration on the question of a global ethic. This declaration, the origin of which is described by Dr Christel Hasselmann in her contribution, is a point at which complex global efforts at inter-religious dialogue and comparative research into religions crystallize. Here is evidence that regardless of the claims to truth that they continue to maintain, religions can from their own sources of faith make an effort to make the ambivalence of the process of economic globalization visible by referring to the resources of the religions in their spirituality and wisdom and by mobilizing forces against a takeover on the one hand and relativism on the other. Dr Günther Gebhardt shows how impressively the Chicago Global Ethic Declaration was developed at the Assembly of the Parliament of the World's Religions in Cape Town in 1999 and implemented in the face of global challenges.

Part II contains contributions from the perspectives of fundamental theology and ethics. It opens with a reflection by the moral theologian Hille Haker on the motive of compassion as a global programme for Christianity projected by J. B. Metz. While this is a religious motif, it can be translated into an ethical concept. Then follows a contribution by Francis Schüssler Fiorenza on questions of universal justice in relation to pluralism and cultural autonomy.

Part III contains contributions towards the application of universal values. Hans Küng and Friedhelm Hengsbach, one indebted to a Christian ecumenical theology and the other to a Christian social ethic, analyse in different approaches the problems of the global economy in the age of globalization, especially the problems of the international networks of trade and the international financial markets. Both are concerned to demystify globalization and discover the real balances of power by reflecting on social ethics in the interest of the well-being of humankind and asking about possible real improvements. Though they both have different approaches to the problem of the global economy and put forward different views, they agree that an improvement of the social situation in many countries cannot come about without constructing international treaties and without strengthening or change in international institutions. Whereas Hans Küng argues that the global market economy achieves its effect only when it is based on an intact democratic civil society which has its foundations in basic values and fundamental standards, Friedhelm Hengsbach emphasizes the importance of the critical public character of the NGOs; these ensure that a global public consciousness comes into being and takes form in global agents in civil society like Amnesty International, Greenpeace, the trade unions and the local churches. Just as important in this context are the reflections by the

Protestant expert on religious education, Johannes Lähnemann, on the practical implementation of the idea of an ethic of humankind for a programme of inter-cultural and inter-religious learning.

Our documentation section has two parts. It seemed important to us in the first part to reflect the theme of universal values in a concrete case relating to medicine and health in an inter-cultural and inter-religious perspective. The medical specialist Dr Ilhan Ilkilic reflects as a Muslim on the theme of the autonomy of the patient, which at present is being much discussed, and the consequences of it for a Muslim patient in a society with pluralist values. The Muslim tradition too, in connection with norms and values, faces the fundamental problem of universality and particularity. People who come from different cultures and live in different cultures must live with this tension in their own consciences, a tension which often subjects their own identity to a hard test.

The second part bears the title 'Whither Moral Theology?' and examines the specific practice of the Catholic magisterium and its refusal to discuss questions with a moral background. The Roman notification issued against our former *Concilium* colleague Marciano Vidal makes it clear that despite the words of the pope quoted in Part I the church finds it difficult to consider the common universal values from the perspective of research.

I. Churches and Religions in Search of Universal Values

Towards a Common Ethical Code for Humankind

Address to the Pontifical Academy of Social Sciences 2001

JOHN PAUL II

Ladies and Gentlemen of the Pontifical Academy of Social Sciences:

1. Your President has just expressed your pleasure at being here in the Vatican to address a subject of concern to both the social sciences and the Magisterium of the Church. I thank you, Professor Malinvaud, for your kind words, and I thank all of you for the help you are generously giving the Church in your fields of competence. For the Seventh Plenary Session of the Academy you have decided to discuss in greater depth the theme of globalization, with particular attention to its ethical implications.

Since the collapse of the collectivist system in Central and Eastern Europe, with its subsequent important effects on the Third World, humanity has entered a new phase in which the market economy seems to have conquered virtually the entire world. This has brought with it not only a growing interdependence of economies and social systems, but also a spread of novel philosophical and ethical ideas based on the new working and living conditions now being introduced in almost every part of the world. The Church carefully examines these new facts in the light of the principles of her social teaching. In order to do this, she needs to deepen her objective knowledge of these emerging phenomena. That is why the Church looks to your work for the insights which will make possible a better discernment of the ethical issues involved in the globalization process.

2. The globalization of commerce is a complex and rapidly evolving phenomenon. Its prime characteristic is the increasing elimination of barriers to the movement of people, capital and goods. It enshrines a kind of triumph of the market and its logic, which in turn is bringing rapid changes in social systems and cultures. Many people, especially the disadvantaged, experience this as something that has been forced upon them, rather than as a process in which they can actively participate.

In my Encyclical Letter *Centesimus Annus*, I noted that the market economy is a way of adequately responding to people's economic needs while respecting their free initiative, but that it had to be controlled by the community, the social body with its common good (cf. nos. 34, 58). Now that commerce and communications are no longer bound by borders, it is the universal common good which demands that control mechanisms should accompany the inherent logic of the market. This is essential in order to avoid reducing all social relations to economic factors, and in order to protect those caught in new forms of exclusion or marginalization.

Globalization, a priori, is neither good nor bad. It will be what people make of it. No system is an end in itself, and it is necessary to insist that globalization, like any other system, must be at the service of the human person; it must serve solidarity and the common good.

3. One of the Church's concerns about globalization is that it has quickly become a cultural phenomenon. The market as an exchange mechanism has become the medium of a new culture. Many observers have noted the intrusive, even invasive, character of the logic of the market, which reduces more and more the area available to the human community for voluntary and public action at every level. The market imposes its way of thinking and acting, and stamps its scale of values upon behaviour. Those who are subjected to it often see globalization as a destructive flood threatening the social norms which had protected them and the cultural points of reference which had given them direction in life.

What is happening is that changes in technology and work relationships are moving too quickly for cultures to respond. Social, legal and cultural safeguards – the result of people's efforts to defend the common good – are vitally necessary if individuals and intermediary groups are to maintain their centrality. But globalization often risks destroying these carefully built up structures, by exacting the adoption of new styles of working, living and organizing communities. Likewise, at another level, the use made of discoveries in the biomedical field tend to catch legislators unprepared. Research itself is often financed by private groups and its results are commercialized even before the process of social control has had a chance to respond. Here we face a Promethean increase of power over human nature, to the point that the human genetic code itself is measured in terms of costs and benefits. All societies recognize the need to control these developments and to make sure that new practices respect fundamental human values and the common good.

4. The affirmation of the priority of ethics corresponds to an essential requirement of the human person and the human community. But not all forms of ethics are worthy of the name. We are seeing the emergence of patterns of ethical thinking which are by-products of globalization itself and which bear the stamp of utilitarianism. But ethical values cannot be dictated by technological innovations, engineering or efficiency; they are grounded in the very nature of the human person. Ethics cannot be the justification or legitimation of a system, but rather the safeguard of all that is human in any system. Ethics demands that systems be attuned to the needs of man, and not that man be sacrificed for the sake of the system. One evident consequence of this is that the ethics committees now usual in almost every field should be completely independent of financial interests, ideologies and partisan political views.

The Church on her part continues to affirm that ethical discernment in the context of globalization must be based upon two inseparable principles:

- First, the inalienable value of the human person, source of all human rights and every social order. The human being must always be an end and not a means, a subject and not an object, nor a commodity of trade.
- Second, the value of human cultures, which no external power has the right to downplay and still less to destroy. Globalization must not be a new version of colonialism. It must respect the diversity of cultures which, within the universal harmony of peoples, are life's interpretive keys. In particular, it must not deprive the poor of what remains most precious to them, including their religious beliefs and practices, since genuine religious convictions are the clearest manifestation of human freedom.

As humanity embarks upon the process of globalization, it can no longer do without a common code of ethics. This does not mean a single dominant socio-economic system or culture which would impose its values and its criteria on ethical reasoning. It is within man as such, within universal humanity sprung from the Creator's hand, that the norms of social life are to be sought. Such a search is indispensable if globalization is not to be just another name for the absolute relativization of values and the homogenization of lifestyles and cultures. In all the variety of cultural forms, universal human values exist and they must be brought out and emphasized as the guiding force of all development and progress.

5. The Church will continue to work with all people of good will to ensure that the winner in this process will be humanity as a whole, and not just a wealthy élite that controls science, technology, communication and the planet's resources to the detriment of the vast majority of its people. The Church earnestly hopes that all the creative elements in society will cooperate to promote a globalization which will be at the service of the whole person and of all people.

With these thoughts, I encourage you to continue to seek an ever deeper insight into the reality of globalization, and as a pledge of my spiritual closeness I cordially invoke upon you the blessings of Almighty God.

The Need for a Global Ethic

Declaration by the Eighth General Assembly in Harare 1998

WORLD COUNCIL OF CHURCHES

1. As we meet today as the eighth assembly of the World Council of Churches, my mind goes back to the second assembly of the WCC in Evanston, in 1954. Meeting at a time of fear and despair, and confrontation between East and West, the assembly made an urgent appeal to the churches and the world 'to turn from our ways to God's way' and 'rejoice in hope'.[1]

These words are more than appropriate forty-four years later at this critical point of history as we come together under darker clouds of uncertainty and hopelessness, in a world threatened ecologically, spiritually and morally, to challenge the churches and the world to
Turn to God – Rejoice in Hope.

2. Unprecedented and far-reaching changes have marked the history of humankind since we met in Canberra (1991). Ideologies have collapsed, barriers have been destroyed, apartheid has almost disappeared. Yet, the end of the cold war has not ushered in a new era of justice, peace and reconciliation. The world remains broken, divided, threatened. These radical and rapid changes and the emergence of complex realities have had direct repercussions in the life and witness of the churches, the ecumenical movement and the work of the WCC.

3. For the Council, the time between Canberra and Harare was marked by a whole series of significant successes in the work of the programme, considerable growth in the membership of the Council, acute financial instability and many different demands from churches and societies. Despite gigantic and unforeseeable difficulties the Council has continued its work, aware of its responsibility and accountability within the framework of the mandate given it by the General Assembly in Canberra. Before I go on to speak of the work of the Council proper I would like to remind you all in a moment of silent prayer of the 'great cloud' of witnesses who came from different

churches and regions and with their important contributions furthered
ecumenical values and goals. These ecumenical witnesses will always be
around us on our shared ecumenical pilgrimage. The work of the Council is
an indivisible whole in which all have a share and to which all make their
particular contribution as individuals or as groups. At this point I would like
to express my warmest thanks and deep appreciation in the name of the
Deputy President and in my own name to the former General Secretary
Dr Emilio Castro, the then General Secretary Dr Konrad Raiser, and all
members of the departing Central Committee and Executive Committees,
the commissions, committees and working groups and the staff of the
Council, which have made such an essential contribution to the implementation of the programme and the study processes which the General Assembly
in Canberra set out.

. . .

70. We belong to one *oikos* or *oikoumene* (household). We are concerned with
the economics (*oikos-nomos*), the management of our common household.

   We are committed to the development of a basic common ethics that
may lead societies from mere existence to meaningful co-existence, from
confrontation to reconciliation, from degeneration of moral values to the
restoration of the quality of life that restores the presence of transcendence
in human life. Global culture must be sustained by a global ethics that will
guide the relations of nations with each other and with the creation, and will
help them to work together for genuine world community. Such a global
ethics, the idea of which was launched by the Parliament of the World's
Religions in 1993 should not reflect the Western Christian ethos; it must be
based on a diversity of experiences and convictions. The church, together
with other living faiths, should seek a global ethics based on shared ethical
values that transcend religious beliefs and narrow definitions of national
interests. Human rights must be undergirded by ethical principles. Therefore, dialogue among religions and cultures is crucial as the basis for greater
solidarity for justice and peace, human rights and dignity. Religions must
work together to identify areas and modes of co-operation in human rights
advocacy. In the thinking surrounding the creation of a global ethics, the
following points must be given due consideration:

   a) We must develop a culture of active non-violence by transforming
structures that generate violence and injustice. The WCC Programme to
Overcome Violence has been engaged in the last few years in the formidable
task of challenging and overcoming the spirit, logic and practice of violence

by transforming the global culture of violence into a culture of just peace. The Peace to the City campaign is a concrete example of people working together as real partners with religions and other groups and movements. In its human rights work the WCC must accompany the struggling communities by encouraging them to act and by building networks between them for collective action. To overcome violence we must address both its causes and its symptoms.

b) Building peace with justice must become a global strategy. Human rights form the essential basis for a just and permanent peace. We must create local, national and international mechanisms and networks that can enhance the peaceful settlement of disputes. We must search for ways to move human rights work from the reactive approach of defending people whose rights are violated to the proactive activity of building and empowering communities that are able to advocate and defend their own rights. National security must be replaced by common security, national interests by common interests: justice for all, peace for all, security for all. This effort should constitute not just a strategy, but a basic ethical principle. At the Seoul JPIC convocation, the WCC affirmed its commitment to seeking every possible means of establishing justice, achieving peace and solving conflicts by active non-violence. Religions, with their inner spiritual resources, can offer opportunities for repentance, forgiveness and reconciliation.

c) We must build a culture of human rights that will provide a constructive and responsible use of power. Often, democratic institutions legitimize power, rather than serving the needs of people. Any expression or use of power that does not carry with it responsibility and accountability is a source of evil. Power becomes a liberating force when it is geared towards justice, encourages participation in social, economic and political institutions and promotes inclusiveness and democracy in the structures of governance.

71. In the *oikoumene* of God there can be no exclusion, no violation of human rights and dignity. We must work for an ethics that offers a new vision of global convergence in order to check the destructive consequences of globalization, technology and secularization, an ethics that promotes a culture of solidarity and the just sharing of resources, an ethics that is not based on charitable philanthropy but on justice. Therefore, let us 'turn to God' who in Christ recreated and liberated humanity as a community to be united under his reign, and who requires that humanity live as a coherent, just and responsible society in the perspective of the kingdom.

Turn to God – Rejoice in Hope.

72. In Amsterdam the churches focussed their attention on 'Man's Disorder and God's Design'. Are we not facing, after fifty years, an even more complex human disorder with still more far-reaching consequences? Can we change the course of history? Can we propose new alternatives to ideological and socio-economic systems and structures that generate injustice, de-humanize societies and jeopardize the integrity and sustainability of creation? We must 'point to God's kingdom', as Karl Barth stated at the Amsterdam assembly, and 'turn to God' to discern God's design for the world today. In fact, turning to God and pointing to God's kingdom is never passive and defensive. It requires sacrificial engagement in God's mission, which is essentially for transforming the whole of humanity and the creation in the perspective of the kingdom. Therefore,

Let us turn to God, and in God let us turn to our fellow human beings.

Note

1. W. A. Visser 't Hooft (ed), *The Evanston Report: The Second Assembly of the World Council of Churches, 1954*, London: SCM Press 1955, p.1.

Global Order and Global Ethic*

'Our world is experiencing a fundamental crisis: a crisis in global economy, global ecology, and global politics.' So begins the Declaration Toward a Global Ethic which was signed in September 1993 by those who took part in the Parliament of the World's Religions in Chicago.

I. No human rights without a basic moral consensus

The present crisis is the consequence of the globalization of almost all spheres of life which has taken place in the last two generations. However, the *de facto* globalization which has come about above all as a result of economic interdependence is not matched by any viable and recognized world order. International law and the international organizations are proving too weak to stem the destructive effects of rapid globalization and keep them under control. The end of the Cold War and the collapse of the bipolar system of stabilization through two great powers has brought the simmering crisis to boiling point.

How can the new world order which is so urgently necessary come about? The question itself is not new. For more than three hundred years, i.e. since the rise of the system of sovereign nation states at the end of the Thirty Years' War, efforts have been made to create a legal framework for relations between states. The two World Wars in our century helped to advance these efforts decisively. They led to the various conventions of humanitarian international law like the Geneva Convention; the basic agreements on working conditions; and above all the institutions of the League of Nations and the United Nations. In its preamble, the United Nations Charter indicates that it is no longer just concerned with ordering relationships between states. Individuals themselves, 'we, the peoples of the United Nations', are the subject of this order, which is founded on belief in the basic values of humanity, in the dignity and value of the human person, and in the equal rights of men and women and of all nations, great or small. The order is to preserve future generations from the scourge of war and to advance justice and social progress in greater freedom. The Universal Declaration on Human Rights of December 1948 formulates the common view of the rights and freedoms of all human beings as the common ideal to be attained by all peoples and nations.

Important though these elements of a world order are, they have not been able to prevent the global crisis. The flagrant violation of human rights in all parts of the world shows that the present international order is more a community of interests of the powerful, and is not primarily orientated on protecting the living conditions of ordinary people. Human rights still remain an ideal without the character of a binding obligation, and their universality is increasingly put in question.

The Declaration Toward a Global Ethic says, 'No new global order without a new global ethic'. Indeed, we know from the experience of developments within society that legislation without a basic moral consensus, regardless of its foundation, can easily become an instrument for the sheer exercise of power and therefore loses its legitimacy. The Universal Declaration on Human Rights was presumably understood by its authors as an expression of such a basic moral consensus. It was an expression of the basic moral values of Western bourgeois culture which in the course of the Enlightenment and secularization had become detached from the authoritative precepts of a morality grounded in the church and religion. The progressive individualization of living conditions and the overwhelming power of instrumental, utilitarian thinking has meanwhile come to undermine this moral consensus, too.

The same processes which as a result have led to the present global crisis are also the cause of the dissolution of the fabric of individual and social morality. Illuminating though the call is for a global ethic as a moral foundation of a new global order, it threatens to run into the sand in the face of the global crisis in all human societies which is becoming visible in the course of globalization.

II. A new moral culture

From the start, the ecumenical movement which has developed among Christian churches since the beginning of this century aimed not only to overcome the historical divisions between the Christian churches but also to build an international order which was to preserve peace between the nations and bring about justice, freedom and respect for human dignity. The ecumenical discussions of the 1920s and 1930s on the construction of international law and the ecumenical contributions to the formulation of the

Charter of the United Nations and the Universal Declaration on Human Rights were based on the conviction that an international legal order had to be rooted in an international ethos, a common basis of moral principles.

For a long time it was presupposed in these discussions that Christianity as a religion with a universal scope and not limited by rational or cultural barriers was the only force which could hold the world together with its moral principles. At the same time, it was expected that Christian culture with its moral foundations would establish itself all over the world as traditional forms of life were displaced.

A process of profound rethinking has taken place over the last thirty years. The churches in an ecumenical movement which is now really world-wide have become aware of their status as a minority in a pluralistic religious world. Moreover, many churches exist as tiny minorities in societies the moral basis of which is determined by other cultural and religious traditions. In this situation there must be a new critical reflection on the universal claim of a Christian ethic.

However, the originally positive view of an international order on the basis of a Christian ethic was shattered from another side. In the course of de-colonialization and the wars of liberation and independence, the global order which had been handed down was increasingly strongly felt to be a decisive hindrance to the realization of justice and peace. Development, it was now said, means change and thus disorder. In view of the signs of a global crisis affecting not only the social order but also the very foundations of morality, ecumenical concerns have meanwhile increasingly been directed towards the reconstruction and safeguarding of the criteria and values which are decisive for preserving the life of human beings and nature. Hence the call for a 'new global system' which is orientated on the demands of justice, peace and the preservation of creation, which respects the cultural and spiritual multiplicity of human societies and takes account of the realities of life. Here it is clear that the issue is not just one of basic values but the development of a new form of life, a 'culture' of non-violence and reverence for life, a culture of dialogue and solidarity.

The attempts to formulate basic convictions and criteria on which such a new moral culture could be orientated go back to biblical Christian traditions. Thus they follow not so much the methods of ethical discourse, but rather a way which is indicated in the biblical tradition itself, of the presentation of collective symbols and stories in which knowledge of the conditions of successful life have been expressed. Here the concern is not so much to inculcate moral norms as an expression of the will of God as to indicate a way and the limits of possible deviations from it. This is taking place in the awareness that Christians everywhere live alongside people who have been shaped by other cultural and religious traditions and derive their moral orientation from them. The experience of interfaith dialogue in mixed communities shows that a mutual recognition is possible which preserves the integrity of each tradition and recognizes the conditions for successful life.

III. What is the status and scope of a global ethic?

The Declaration Toward a Global Ethic goes one stage further. It seeks to root the vision of the peaceful co-existence of peoples in justice and freedom through an order safeguarded by law, which is expressed in the Universal Declaration on Human Rights, in a 'fundamental consensus on binding values, irrevocable standards, and personal attitudes'. It is confident that the different religious and ethical traditions of humankind contain sufficient elements of an ethic 'which is convincing and practical for all women and men of good will, religious and non-religious'. To some degree the Declaration attempts to make mutual recognition visible in the conditions of successful life and to maintain its central insights.

This leads to a simple and convincing basic structure. Starting from the basic conviction that 'Every human being must be treated humanely', which has been expressed in the Golden Rule known in almost all religions and ethical traditions, the Declaration identifies four 'irrevocable directives':

- You shall not kill! Or in positive terms: Have respect for life!
- You shall not steal! Or in positive terms: Deal honestly and fairly!
- You shall not lie! Or in positive terms: Speak and act truthfully!
- You shall not commit sexual immorality! Or in positive terms: Respect and love one another!

These directives aim at a culture of non-violence, solidarity, tolerance and equal rights.

In the background of this structure we can clearly recognize a recollection of the biblical traditions, especially the 'second table' of the Decalogue. But it also seeks to contribute towards the renewal of the spiritual and moral forces of the other religious traditions. The Declaration wishes 'to recall irrevocable, unconditional ethical norms. These should not be bonds and chains, but helps and supports for people to find and realize once again in their lives directions, orientations, and meaning.' The ultimate aim of the Declaration is to encourage that change of awareness without which the global crisis cannot be overcome and our world cannot be changed for the better.

The close relationship between the Declaration and the ecumenical quest mentioned earlier is unmistakable. In both instances the concern is the reconstruction of a culture which enhances life by recalling directives which have become concealed and relating them to the present day. The decisive difference is that the Declaration makes the claim to formulate elements of a global ethic which is clear to all men and women of good will, one that they can live out and is therefore also binding. The insight, veiled by experience, that no society can survive without a basic ethical consensus becomes the postulate: No new global order without a global ethic and its expression in the formulation of irrevocable unconditional ethical norms.

But is this conclusion convincing? Does what applies to each closed society apply in the same way to the global society? What is the status and scope of the 'global ethic' formulated here? Is it really meant to be normative, or rather 'regulative', in the sense of furthering mutual recognition and a change of awareness, i.e. initiating a process of common searching and understanding?

Any ethic that can be lived out is embedded in cultural and religious traditions. Moral awareness is formed through symbols, stories and rituals, which are handed down from one generation to the next. The root of any morality that can be lived out is a concrete community of people, their history, their traditions, their interpretation of the world. Ethics are like language: we can learn the rules for translation from one language to another, but the rules themselves do not produce a global language.

The Declaration Toward a Global Ethic formulates more the rules which can help in the process of mutual knowledge in the awareness of successful life. They can help to revive concealed knowledge and thus be a stimulus towards a change of awareness. However, the validity and binding nature of the directives can be grounded only in the different concrete contexts of traditions. This remains the limitation of any 'global ethic'.

IV. Towards a fundamental change of awareness

Discussion on the Declaration Toward a Global Ethic has gone on. It has prompted a broad response, not least in economic and political circles. Working with Hans Küng, in 1997 the InterAction Council presented a 'Universal Declaration of Human Responsibilities' in which the idea of a global ethic is related to action in economic and political contexts worldwide. The World Economic Forum in Davos also took up the impetus.

Hans Küng in particular has continued to work on the basic issues with the Global Ethic Foundation which he has established. The two volumes,

Hans Küng, *A Global Ethic for Global Politics and Economics*, London and
New York 1997, and Hans Küng and Karl-Josef Kuschel (eds), *Wissenschaft
und Weltethos*, Munich 1998, are an impressive testimony to this work.
There can be no doubt about the fruitfulness of the debate which he has
started.

The inter-religious dialogue at a world level has been markedly intensified, above all since the publication of the Declaration of the Parliament of
the World's Religions in 1993. The Parliament itself further developed the
framework marked out by the Declaration at its conference in Cape Town in
1999. The Declaration has been referred to with approval in many church
and inter-religious gatherings at a world level. At all events the process of a
common search and agreement on ethical principles has got under way. And
it is more urgent than ever, if S. Huntington's forecast of a 'clash of civiliza-
tions' is not to come true.

However, the questions about the status and scope of the Global Ethic
Declaration which I formulated in 1995 remain, and they can now be made
more precise by making a comparison with another project of similar focus,
the Earth Charter, which was presented officially in the Hague in 2000. The
Earth Charter goes back to a suggestion in the 1987 Brundtland Report
on environment and development. The environmental summit in Rio de
Janeiro 1992 came to grief over the attempt to formulate a charter. Now,
after a long process of discussion, there is a text which is to be distributed in
2002, ten years after the environmental summit, to the General Assembly of
the United Nations for its approval.

This is not the place to present the Charter, with its sixteen principles and
sixty concrete examples. The intention of the four responsibilities with
which it is prefaced is very close to the four directives of the Global Ethic
Declaration. However, where the Global Declaration has as a preface
the Golden Rule as a basic ethical conviction and thus remains within the
anthropocentric horizon of the ethical traditions of the great religions, the
Earth Charter begins with the community of all life. Both agree in the quest
for a global order which is based on reverence of life, universal respect for
human rights, economic justice and a culture of peace and non-violence.

The decisive difference is that the Global Ethic Declaration is a text by
'experts', drafted against the background of and with reference to the
authority of the great religious traditions, whereas the Earth Charter
presents itself as a text which came into being out of a broad dialogue on
shared aims and values. Presumably the formulation of the Earth Charter is
a model for a really open and participatory process involving individuals and
organizations from all regions, cultures and religious traditions. It expresses

the expectations and hopes of the civil society which is slowly taking shape at a global level.

Both the Global Ethic Declaration and the Earth Charter call for a fundamental change of awareness. However, the Earth Charter remains deliberately secular: it is based only on the evidence and the manifest truth of the ethical demands which it formulates. Thus it is the expression of a public discussion and seeks to expand this basis.

By contrast, the Global Ethic Declaration is based on the validity of the great religious traditions and their claim to truth. It too is ultimately aimed at reception, i.e. at assent and a process of dialogue. It can prepare rules of agreement but it cannot usher in the change of awareness. The Global Ethic Declaration is as much a challenge to the great religions as a consensus on fundamental value orientations which has already been achieved. It offers the religions a common language with which they can begin to respond to the challenges of the twenty-first century.

A 'global culture' must grow from below. Therefore the two approaches are complementary and it is to be hoped that they bring about the necessary change of awareness.

Translated by John Bowden

*Editors' note: sections I–III derive from a contribution which Konrad Raiser made in 1995 to the Volume *Yes to a Global Ethic*, ed. Hans Küng, London and New York 1996. Section IV has been added for *Concilium*.

The 1993 Chicago Global Ethic Declaration

The Parliament of the World's Religions

CHRISTEL HASSELMANN

I. The task and significance of the global ethic

People first became aware of the existence of the global ethic when it was presented in the Declaration Toward a Global Ethic at the Parliament of the World's Religions in Chicago in 1993. The Parliament, which has also been called 'the second Parliament of the World's Religions', was held between 28 August and 4 September and was convened for two reasons. First, there was to be a celebration of the centenary of the first Parliament, and secondly, the representatives of the world religions were to meet to discuss the problems of the world. Up to that point it was the greatest meeting of representatives of the world religions in world history. The council of the second Parliament of the World Religions had for the first time ventured to work out a declaration on a global ethic. The Declaration Toward a Global Ethic is the first document of this nature in the thousands of years of the history of religion. It is the result of a draft by Hans Küng and consultation with over two hundred scholars, who represent the faith communities of the world. In the Declaration Toward a Global Ethic, which was ceremonially proclaimed at the Parliament of the World's Religions in 1993, Küng developed a vision in which the representatives of the world religions commit themselves to observing the common ethical foundation of all religions. After it was approved at the Parliament, the Declaration was read by around forty million people.

In view of the crisis threatening human survival and planet earth, according to Küng it is the religions who have a special role in the quest for a new world order. His starting point is that the destructive potential of the religions which has manifested itself in history so far can be reversed, that the international community cannot exist without common values, and that an alliance over ethics could prove a bond which would unite the community of nations and be a basis for peace. That is new, in that for centuries – down to the present day – there has been and often still is not only ignorance but also hostility and intolerance. Now in working out the Global Ethic Declaration and its approval at the Parliament of the World's Religions Küng has made a twofold breakthrough:

- For the first time, with the awareness of a planetary responsibility on the part of the world religions, a common aim for co-operation in the world community has been developed.
- With the Declaration Toward a Global Ethic, a shared ethical consensus has been created on which this collaboration can build.

Four 'great directives of humankind', a practical code of behaviour which applies in all the great world religions, form the core of the global ethic: you shall not kill, steal, lie or commit adultery. They can be called the Magna Carta of a universal ethic of humankind. In addition there are two basic directives: 'Every human being must be treated humanely' and the Golden Rule ('What you do not wish done to you, do not do to others'). With the help of the mathematical concept of the intersection (an area of ethical overlap), the global ethic can be defined as 'the part of the ethical core of a religion which it shares with all other religions'. The Declaration makes the claim to be the ethical foundation for a new world order. But what is to be understood by a new world order? The new world order has in view a world in which people are aware that the earth belongs to all and that human beings – also as individuals – are responsible for it. They are aware that the economy of greed must be changed into an economy of community. There is an awareness that every nation can thrive only when it takes account of and furthers the prosperity of the other nations. There is an awareness that the word 'we' embraces humankind and all life on this planet. For this, collaboration and a shared ethical consensus are needed.

The reactions of the representatives of the world religions have shown that the particular ethical values within the religious and spiritual traditions, which so far have hardly been discovered, are riches with which the critical problems of the world could be addressed. At the same time, the signatures of the religious leaders of the world religions show that an agreement on an ethical consensus which transcends cultures and extends over religions is possible. Awareness of this first came about with the Declaration. The signatories include the Buddhist Dalai Lama and the Catholic Cardinal Archbishop of Chicago, along with rabbis, leading Muslims, Hindus and representatives of lesser religions.

II. Two levels of development: the Parliament and the Global Ethic Declaration

We must imagine two ways leading towards the Declaration Toward a Global Ethic. First of all there is the basis of inter-religious dialogue on which the Declaration builds. The beginning of this can demonstrably be traced back to the first Parliament in Chicago in 1893. The second is the four-year phrase of the real preparation of the Global Ethic Declaration. The two levels are closely connected. It can be demonstrated that since the first Parliament of the World's Religions in 1893 there has been a change in awareness in the perception of the pluralism of the world religions which has acted as a signal. With the development of a minimal ethical consensus – the Declaration Toward a Global Ethic – and its presentation and approval at the second Parliament of the World's Religions in 1993, this change of awareness has reached a historical climax, the effect of which has still to be seen.

1. Dialogue as a bridge linking the world religions

The first Parliament of the World's Religions in Chicago in 1893 was the first formal meeting of the representatives of the world's religions in world history. It has gone down in the history of the world's religions as an important event, as 'the dawn of religious pluralism'. At the same time it is the '"introduction" of Asian religions to the West'[1] and expresses the beginning of an inter-religious dialogue and at the same time the beginning of a new century 'in the course of which we all became neighbours'.[2] A contemporary described the memorable event as 'perhaps the most important religious gathering that ever took place'.[3] The Parliament evaluated the event as 'a new age in the evolution of religious life for the world',[4] and the 'father of the study of religion', Friedrich Max Müller (1823–1900), called it 'one of the most memorable events in world history'.[5]

Although important religious communities (e.g. Islam), the 'hardliners' of the religions and whole parts of the earth were not represented at all, the congress bore fruit: concrete evidence of the change of awareness is given by the dates of the formation of inter-religious organizations. Whereas the dialogue between the religions had its spectacular beginning in Chicago in 1893 with the 'Parliament of the World's Religions', only seven years later the 'International Association for Religious Freedom' (IARF) was founded in Boston. It is the oldest inter-religious organization which still exists, and participants in the Parliament were among its founders. Other organizations followed. Especially in the period after the Second World War, the inter-religious dialogue developed into a movement which put down roots in many countries, forced on by migrations and travels. National and international organizations like the World Congress of Faiths (WCF), the Temple of Understanding (TOU) and the World Conference on Religion and Peace (WCRP), along with the Interfaith Centre in Oxford, established themselves and took on the task of overcoming the traditional relationship between the religions, stamped by the spirit of exclusivism and opposition to reconciliation. The religions were to be led out of their isolation in strongholds and to co-operate for the good of all humankind.

After the Parliament the presence of Eastern religions in the USA and Europe also began. The world religions were brought together. Around eighty years after the 1893 Parliament, the 'Guidelines for Inter-religious Dialogue' laid down by the World Council of Churches gave impetus to 'official' inter-religious dialogue, dialogue between the religious institutions. The Second Vatican Council gave a further important impetus to a change of awareness with the 'Declaration on the Relation of the Church to Non-Christian Religions'. The key sentence runs: 'The Catholic Church rejects nothing of what is true and holy in these religions.'[6] However, the question arises whether the Council – in the face of the pluralization of society, the development of democracy and the claim of other religions to equality – was not reacting a century late to a practical necessity in a way which would have been appropriate to the situation described after 1893 rather than to the requirements and challenges of the galloping globalization of *our* time.[7]

Although in the last hundred years there have been valuable impulses towards a change of awareness and active peace work at inter-religious meetings, the magnitudes of the issue must not be lost sight of. Most people know absolutely nothing about the collaboration between the religions. Encounters take place either at an official level between religious institutions or at the level of the inter-religious organizations and other bodies of equal status. But at the level of the 'average citizen' we frequently find ignorance, indifference and a lack of readiness to look beyond the limits of one's own religion, and also uncertainty and fear of anything alien.

2. *The origin of the Global Ethic Declaration*

The Global Ethic Declaration arose out of two quite separate developments in America and Europe which finally came together with the approval of the Declaration in the final session of the Parliament of the World's Religions in 1993. In America a group of those interested in relations between the

religions had formed to organize the second Parliament of the World's
Religions, and at the same time in Germany Hans Küng had worked on an
idea which he called the 'Global Ethic Project'. The organizers of the
Parliament and Küng met in 1989, when Küng was talking about his concern at the University of Chicago. The Council of the Parliament thereupon
gave Küng the task of working out the draft of a 'Declaration of the Religions
Toward a Global Ethic'. Küng was thus venturing on a problematical
undertaking: for the first time in the history of the religions an ethical declaration was to be worked out which was to be acceptable to the members of all
the religions of the world. There were no historical precedents.

A series of questions were connected with this problem, the answers to
which will be described in my work. What should such a declaration look
like? What claims were put to it? What linguistic form should it be given?
And above all what values, irrevocable criteria and inner basic attitudes
capable of a consensus should it be given? The following further questions
stand at the centre of my investigation. What did Küng's initial reflections
on a first ethical consensus look like? The initial spark came with the basic
paper which Küng wrote in 1989 for a UNESCO organization and the
reactions to it from the world religions. Further stages of development are
Küng's lecture to the World Economic Forum in Davos in 1990, his best-
seller *Global Responsibility*, the results of a Tübingen course in 1992, and
written statements by individuals and groups on the individual drafts. What
comments, suggestions for change and criticism were made on the drafts and
what effect did they have on the text of the Declaration?

After Küng had received the first critical response on his idea as a result
of his 1989 UNESCO paper, stimulation came above all from the 1992
colloquium, which he took into account. It was his intention that the
Declaration should be primarily a declaration of the religions, to be followed
later by a more general one. It aims at a consensus, and out of respect for the
Buddhists refrains from speaking 'in the name of God'. The ethical levels of
the binding values, criteria and attitudes stand at the centre. At the same
time the Declaration had to be capable of being understood by anyone, so
that it could be translated.

We should note that the focal point of Küng's argument is the close connection between global ethic, human rights and world peace. After evaluat-
ing the reactions from the world religions and the consultations with experts
it can be concluded that in principle the working out of a global ethic is
important for world peace. Nevertheless many questions and also objections
were raised. They included the problem of translation and the question of
the unity of the religions, and the fear that Western culture would be too

prominent. Despite deep objections, it can be said that these problems could not be ignored, but that in the end they did not pose any insuperable obstacles.

Although representatives of the individual religious communities confirm that the *humanum* can be found in all religions, the attempt to connect the world religions with human rights and to identify their basic contribution to the *humanum* with Western humanism was thought to have its problems. It is a risky venture on the part of a Christian theologian (Küng) to invite the representatives of the different religions to reflect on what role human rights play in their own traditions. Negative experiences from history raise the not unfounded suspicion that Christianity wants to assert itself as a model religion which has already taken over human rights theologically for itself and now wants to demonstrate its moral superiority. Against this background, the Global Ethic Declaration also arouses the suspicion that it has been conceived out of, and is associated with, a Christian or at least a 'Western' perspective which has correspondingly inclusivist ambitions. Similarly, one cannot overlook the fact that the Vatican did not support the Declaration on Human Rights by an appropriate resolution, since it is not a member of the United Nations. Only in 1965 did the Catholic Church officially approach the liberal tradition of human rights through the Council Declaration on Religious Freedom.[8] For centuries, human rights were condemned as un-Christian. Now they are no longer seen by representatives of either Catholicism or Protestantism as rivals to the specifically Christian picture of human beings; on the contrary, human rights are adopted as a heritage which makes Christianity specific. Reflecting on this background, one is not surprised that the question is raised whether the claim of the universal validity of human rights is a piece of Western cultural imperialism or whether human rights are culturally neutral. The results of investigations have shown that – despite this objection – the awareness that human rights apply to all is growing in the world.

To some degree the inadequate collaboration of the world religions so far is among the obstacles to making the global ethic concrete. In his three impressive theses Küng therefore calls for rethinking: 'No survival without a global ethic. No world peace without religious peace. No peace among the religions without dialogue between the religions.' Collaboration needs dialogue, which presupposes mutual credibility, honesty and trust. I have investigated all this: it is clearly important that the world 'dialogue' has become a central term in the new perception of other religions. A distinction needs to be made between the dialogue of 'official' religious institutions and the dialogue of the 'unofficial' representatives of the religions. The practice of dialogue is far more developed within the inter-religious organizations than in the religious institutions.

The willingness and capacity of 'official' Christianity for dialogue is judged to be disappointing both by some non-Christian and also by some Christian theologians. Here there is criticism of both the rigid attitude of the churches and also the mixture of mission and dialogue. Through writings from the Vatican and the Protestant Church, through patterns of behaviour down to the present, by means of the self-criticism expressed by competent members of the Christian religion and (vigorous) critical reaction from adherents of non-Christian religions, it can be demonstrated that Christianity adopts an ambivalent attitude to dialogue; not just for altruistic reasons it can be said to be the religion which most actively serves to promote interreligious dialogue. Inclusivist intentions by Christians already made themselves felt at the first Parliament in their the wish to evangelize the world. In the year 2000 the Catholic claim to power was recently renewed in the declaration *Dominus Jesus*. Many adherents of other religions regard these claims of inclusivism and superiority by the churches with mistrust and antipathy. Here historically negative experiences play a heightened role (as we can hear, for example, from Judaism).[9] The rigid attitude of the central authorities of the churches is also criticized by Christian theologians of very different kinds (John Hick, Paul Knitter, etc.) and the call for a kind of 'Copernican shift' is made to provide a basis for international peace. However, the latest development in the relations of the Catholic Church to Judaism represented by the pope's *mea culpa* and his visit to Israel in 2000 indicate a change of course which will go down in history. Furthermore, the great inter-religious congresses which have recently increased in number will perhaps automatically ensure a further contemporary development in the capacity for dialogue on the part of 'official' Christianity and the other conservative and orthodox groups of other religions, which are even more restrained. Here mention should be made, for example, of the world peace summit in New York in the autumn of 2001.

The clarification of the question of truth is *the* cardinal question for Christianity,[10] but the religions of East Asia cannot understand how there could be a dispute over it. In this connection Küng considers three strategies of dialogue more closely: the *fortress strategy*, which assumes that only one's own religion is true and the others are untrue;[11] the *strategy of playing down differences*, in which religious peace is achieved by levelling down and ignoring the differences and contradictions between the religions; and finally the *strategy of embrace*, which sees the other religions only as preliminary stage of its own universal truth and wants to integrate all human beings in this world into the one true religion (inclusivism).[12] After judging all these three dialogue strategies to be unusable and regarding self-criticism by the religions as indispensable, Küng brought the *humanum* to the centre as an ecumenical criterion of truth. This move was vigorously criticized, because it made humanity the criterion (the *humanum* as a supersystem)[13] and not the religion, which was thus degraded from subject to object. In the course of the composition of the Global Ethic Declaration Küng has distanced himself from anything that implies rivalry and evaluation. What could have been referred to in this proposal in a merely marginal way is made the basic demand in the Declaration: 'Every human being must be treated humanely.'[14] It is no longer the theological disputations which ultimately stand at the centre; coping with the problems together unites the religions. This 'purpose-orientated' strategy must be developed even further in the future, since in the end it is the only strategy which not only overcomes the plurality of the religions – without doing away with it – but can even make use of it as a supplementary element.

III. The further development of the global ethic

In the course of their history the world religions have made little contribution towards peace in the world; therefore many theologians doubt their ethical force and whether they can change in a positive direction.[15] The slight optimism about peace among the religions which is shared above all by the monotheistic religions (Judaism, Christianity and Islam) is based on the negative experiences from history and the deeply rooted tendency of religious institutions to ally themselves with the powerful.

As the religions all over the world play a not insignificant role in many violent clashes, Küng's basic presupposition is that the religions could just as well direct their influence in the direction of making peace – if they were ready to rethink. But that raises the question why it should be the religions that provide the ethical basis for a global world order. After all, they have often issued calls for intolerance, violation of human rights and even holy wars. It is the religions which themselves transgress against the commandments that they themselves propagate. Nothing has changed here even now. That Küng, too, realistically has this discrepancy in view is evident from his call in his 1990 Davos speech: 'the religions must show credibly that despite all their errors they are concerned with human well-being'.

The ever-growing large group of the non-religious must not be overlooked.[16] One can point to a chain of significant philosophers and philosophical schools which long before the advent of Christianity and other religions taught a humanistic, rational ethic with a moral foundation and orientated on responsible action.[17] Buddhism refutes assertions that it is difficult to provide a foundation for morality without reference to God and that all religions are to be subsumed under God.

To sum up, it can be said that many tasks still remain in the whole field of religious encounter:

- Although in many spheres (business, politics, culture, sport, etc) the development of an information network is increasing globally, there is comparatively little movement between the religions.
- Although leading figures in the religious communities, inter-religious movements and individual base groups have recognized the need for inter-religious dialogue and co-operation over the questions of human survival, so far the religious communities have not yet grasped this as a whole. They are still concerned with the 'circles around them'. The religions are not yet ready to bear responsibility for the planet together; they are far from having perceived it in all its breadth.
- With a view to the rising generation it should be noted that inter-religious and inter-cultural elements have still not been sufficiently been implemented in the training of teachers.
- The power struggle of the main churches over the religious dimension in schools must no longer use inter-religious and ethical education as a substitute for religious education.[18] The inter-religious and inter-cultural content of various school disciplines must be co-ordinated more consistently and taught in a way which is neutral to any world-view – in other words, as religious studies.

Our spiritual attitude – our view of life and the world – will to a great degree be the decisive factor for the future: for the future of humankind, the future of the environment and the future of the earth. For our action is governed by our thought. 'We take individual responsibility for all we do. All our decisions, actions, and failures have consequences.'[19] Whether children are trained for war – as in some countries of Africa, in Iran and recently in Russia[20] – or for a better understanding and peaceful co-existence on the basis of human rights, as for example in Germany, will influence the spiritual attitude of this young generation and its future. Therefore in my view a fourth sentence should be added to Küng's triad of 'No survival without a global ethic', 'No world peace without religious peace', 'No religious peace without religious dialogue': 'No future without inter-religious education'.

Küng's idea of a global ethic has long been the subject of international political discussion. Küng's 'stone thrown into the water is now making circles'.[21] The global ethic has its place on the global agenda at many international conferences and commissions,[22] and the Global Ethic Foundation is taking pains to further this initiative. In his many books which have appeared since 1993, Küng shows how not only the world religions but also world politics, the world economy and science need a basic ethical orientation which is binding on all. Here he is presenting a concrete basic orientation for a more humane order. Whereas up to the publication of his book *Global Responsibility* (in German in 1990) Küng could hardly refer to any documents of world organizations on a global ethic, only seven years after the proclamation of the Global Ethic Declaration in 1993 there were several important international documents which spoke out not only on human rights but also on human responsibilities, which programmatically called for a global ethic and already attempted to spell it out. A further chink of light was the endorsement of the importance of a global ethic for the first time by the General Assembly of the World Council of Churches in Harare in 1998.[23]

Further important congresses from which closer collaboration between the religions is hoped for were the General Assembly of the World Council of Religions for Peace in Amman, Jordan, at the end of November 1999 and the third Parliament of the World's Religions in Cape Town, South Africa in the first week of December that same year. There is a plan to have a new Parliament of the World's Religions every five years at different places in the world, and a new 'Assembly' of religious and spiritual leaders three years before every Parliament and during the Parliament. The Global Ethic Declaration is to be disseminated and discussed as a basis for mutual understanding. A 'last' version of the document cannot and will not be produced. 'Rather, the process will continue to move "toward a global ethic".'[24]

Great complexes of ethical problems, from genetics, the economy, medicine and ecology to nuclear physics, are a common and ever more urgent challenge to all the world religions. The voice of an individual religious community has long been far too thin. The consensus of testimonies from all the world religions would together produce an immense volume. Therefore inter-religious research and interdisciplinary collaboration (in religious studies, philosophy, theology and the humane and social sciences) could become very important. Here the global ethic forms a minimal ethical basis.

Like a ship in a storm, a ship which contains humankind, the religions have only two possibilities: either they continue their disputes and power claims among one another and do not care if the ship sinks and humankind perishes, or they use their ethical wisdom to supplement and support one another, also bringing in those who are not religious, to join in saving the ship 'Earth'. Should the religions decide for the latter, it would necessarily lead to an unprecedented and enormous revaluation of all the religions – in so far as understanding and harmony prevails between them.

But will the world religions perceive their responsibility in the globalization process at all through the possibility of an approach via the global ethic? Or will they lag behind beaten in the galloping process of globalization? The United Nations declared the year 2000 the International Year for a Culture of Peace. 'Dialogue' is the central point for 2001. But as long as the religious communities do not put an end to the perversion of religion, as long as there are powers for which there are higher values than peace, as long as there are values for the world community which fall silent in the face of war and look on passively, there is little hope of the realization of a vision of peace among humankind. One world or none? There is no alternative. Pope John Paul II put it in an ambiguous way: 'None of us is in a position to foresee the future. But we know that the world will be what we want it to be.'[25]

Translated by John Bowden

Notes

1. Letter from Daniel Gómez-Ibáñez, Executive Director of the Council, to Küng, 2 March 1993.
2. Letter from Gómez-Ibáñez to Küng in December 1991.
3. Leaflet 'General Information' from the Council for a Parliament of the World's Religions, Chicago nd, p.1.
4. Ibid.
5. Marcus Braybrooke, *Pilgrimage of Hope. One Hundred Years of Global Interfaith Dialogue*, London and New York 1992, p.7.
6. Declaration on Relations of the Church with with Non-Christian Religions, 2.
7. It should be noted that Confucians today are all too well aware that no single religious tradition can claim to be the complete embodiment of the truth. And the refusal to acknowledge other truths of faith also seems alienating to Buddhists and Hindus.
8. In 1975 the Vatican signed the CSCE final communiqué, which refers to the United Nations Declaration on Human Rights. The promotion of human rights is emphasized in the 1991 encyclical *Centesimus Annus*.
9. The German Conference of Bishops self-critically recognizes the difficulties: 'The burden of history makes the proclamation all the more difficult when certain methods of evangelization in the past have provoked fear and mistrust on the part of the adherents of other religions.' They 'could fear that the evangelization of the churches could end in the destruction of their own religion and culture'. Statement of the Apostolic See no.102, Papal Council for Inter-Religious Dialogue, Congregation for the Evangelization of the Peoples, German text Bonn 1991.

10. Based on Jesus' saying in John 14.6, 'I am the way, the truth and the life.'
11. This was the traditional Roman Catholic position (*Extra ecclesiam nulla salus* – 'Outside the church no salvation').
12. Cf. H. Küng, *Global Responsibility*, London and New York 1991, pp.78–81.
13. E. Borowitz in H. Küng and K.-J. Kuschel, *Weltfrieden durch Religionsfrieden*, Munich 1993, p.73.
14. H. Küng and K.-J. Kuschel, *A Global Ethic. The Declaration of the Parliament of the World's Religions*, London and New York 1993.
15. In *Yes to a Global Ethic*, London and New York 1995, p.31, Richard von Weizsäcker writes: 'Here the question of the ethical force of the religions becomes central . . . They have often also been damaged by their claims to truth which lead them to live in conflict with one another; the resultant tensions keep being transferred to society as a whole and thus create disturbances as well as peace.'
16. It was given due status in the third Parliament in Cape Town in 1999.
17. Thus for example Protagoras (485–414 BC), without referring to religion, comes to the same conclusion with his maxim 'Man is the measure of all things'. It is not only the Greek philosophers (Socrates, Plato and Aristotle) who have a tremendous potential of ethical wisdom; it can also be found – outside religion – in other cultures, ancient Indian, Chinese, Arab, etc.
18. Cf. Jürgen Lott, *Wie hast du's mit der Religion? Das neue Schulfach 'Lebensgestaltung-Ethik-Religionskunde' (LER) und die Werteerziehung in der Schule*, Gütersloh 1998.
19. *A Global Ethic* (n.14), p.14.
20. See the article 'Russland. Waffenkunde für Schüler', *Der Spiegel* 7/2000, p.146. It quotes from *Isvestiya*: 'The West should understand that Russia still has the power to turn into a military monster in the style of the former Soviet Union.'
21. Cf. Hans Küng and Karl-Josef Kuschel (eds), *Wissenschaft und Weltethos*, Munich 1998, p.13.
22. Mention should be made here of the UN Commission for Global Governance (1995), the Global Commission for Culture and Development (1995), the Valencia Third Millennium Project (1997), the World Economic Forum in Davos (1997), the UNESCO Universal Ethics Project in Paris (1997) and the Sixth Indira Gandhi Conference in Delhi 1997. See Johannes Frühbauer, 'From the Declaration of the Religions to the Declaration of the Statesmen. Stages in the Composition of the Declaration of Human Responsibilities' in H. Küng and H. Schmidt (eds), *A Global Ethic and Global Responsibilities*, London 1998, pp.94–6.
23. Cf. the interview with Küng, 'Leitplanken für die Moral. Der katholische Theologe H. Küng über die Renaissance der soziale Bewegungen und ein Weltethos im Zeitalter der Globalisierung', *Der Spiegel* 51, 1999, p.70.
24. Information from the Council for a Parliament of the World's Religions, no title, Chicago nd, p.3.
25. John Paul II, *Wir fürchten die Wahrheit nicht. Der Papst über die Schuld der Kirche und der Menschen*, Graz, Vienna and Cologne ²1998, p.70.

From Chicago to the 1999 Cape Town Call

GÜNTHER GEBHARDT

I. Chicago 1993: a milestone in the inter-religious movement

The second Parliament of the World's Religions in Chicago in 1993 marks the beginning of a new stage in the movement of inter-religious dialogue which began a century previously, characterized by an intensified orientation on praxis.[1] Those in the religions who are ready for dialogue have recognized that the great problems for the present and future of our planet – peace, justice, human rights, sustainable development, the preservation of the natural environment – concern all human beings equally, simply on the basis of their common humanity. Thus all religions are also involved in a shared destiny and responsibility, and the awareness has developed that they must use their spiritual and ethical resources together in grappling with all these problems. Of course this recognition was not new: as early as 1970 the founding of the World Conference of the Religions for Peace (WCRP) was governed by this impulse.[2] But the quite new perspective which has developed has been the orientation of inter-religious dialogue on practical action as a result of the central event of the Chicago Parliament: the Declaration Toward a Global Ethic, which will be investigated more closely at another point in this issue.[3]

In the evaluation of the Chicago Parliament as a whole, the acceptance of this document, in which a minimal consensus on ethical values, standards and attitudes was again brought to awareness as a common basis of action for all religions and humanistic world-views, is widely regarded as its most important event, one which has far-reaching consequences. The way from Chicago to Cape Town can therefore also be understood as the history of the effect of the Global Ethic Declaration and as a further development of the Global Ethic Project. In the account that follows this will therefore be given pride of place. First of all, however, some subsequent developments in the inter-religious movement since 1993 need to be mentioned.

1. The Council for a Parliament of the World's Religions (CPWR)

This organization, which is based in Chicago, took responsibility for the preparation and organization of the two Parliaments in Chicago and Cape Town. Its activity initially developed in two directions, locally in Chicago itself through a 'Metropolitan Inter-religious Initiative' and internationally through the 'International Inter-religious Initiative'. As well as preparing for parliaments which take place periodically and inter-religious projects for the year 2000, this latter branch within CPWR saw as an essential aspect of its role the dissemination of the Global Ethic Declaration. The Executive Director Jim Kenney is the central figure here, with his indefatigable commitment to the preparation and implementation of the Cape Town Parliament.

2. Subsequent initiatives

But the formation of two new inter-religious organizations, the Peace Council and the United Religions Initiative (URI), are also part of the offshoots of the Chicago Parliament.

The Peace Council stems from the initiative of the former executive Director of CPWR, Daniel Gómez-Ibáñez. In 1995 the Peace Council was founded as a group of high-ranking spiritual and religious authorities like the Dalai Lama and Archbishop Desmond Tutu, who by virtue of their personal moral authority in specific questions of peace represent the voice of the religions, as for example within the campaign against landmines.

The United Religions Initiative (URI) was also founded in 1995; the occasion for this new movement was the inter-religious celebration of the fiftieth anniversary of the foundation of the United Nations in San Francisco. The spiritual leader is the Episcopalian (Anglican) Bishop of California, William Swing. Just as the United Nations Organization is a forum for the peaceful exchange of interests and the collaboration of states, so he envisages a similar forum for the daily peaceful collaboration of the religions, a United Religions Organization. URI understands itself as a process leading towards this goal and attempts in a decentralized way to involve as many people as possible in this process, starting from small grass-roots groups everywhere. In June 2000, after a four-year process of discussion and consultation, a charter was agreed. In it URI defines itself as 'a growing global community dedicated to promoting enduring, daily inter-religious co-operation, ending religiously motivated violence and creating cultures of peace, justice and healing for the Earth and all living beings'. In his booklet *The Coming United Religions*,[4] Bishop Swing welcomes the

Global Ethic Project as a step in the right direction, but thinks that if a global ethic is to be effective, it needs a permanent organization of the religions within which the religions can time and again achieve their ethical consensus. Of course Swing sees URI as the appropriate way towards this goal.

Though all these organizations also take account of the idea of a global ethic in different ways in some of their activities, the decisive breakthrough of the Global Ethic Project towards wider influence only came about after 1993, with the setting up of the Global Ethic Foundation in Tübingen. This also took place in 1995. Because of its central role as the co-ordinating centre for the Global Ethic Project, the Foundation took an active part in the process leading to the third Parliament of the World's Religions.

II. From the Global Ethic Declaration to the Call to Our Guiding Institutions

One of the main tasks of the Council for a Parliament of the World's Religions (CPWR) was and is the organization of Parliaments of the World's Religions at regular intervals. The CPWR convened the third Parliament of the World's Religions at Cape Town in 1999 under the heading 'A New Day Dawning: Spiritual Yearnings and Sacred Possibilities'. Two levels need to be distinguished here.

• The Parliament itself represents a great open public event with thousands of participants offering hundreds of programmes, a colourful kaleidoscope of the inter-religious reality of our world, which includes a great diversity of spiritual groups and individuals.
• At the heart of the Parliament, however, is the 'Assembly of Religious and Spiritual Leaders', called the 'Parliament Assembly' for short. This is a group of figures (in Chicago over two hundred) who as individuals and in part as official representatives of institutions, communities and academic organizations of the religions and spiritual groups, are both invited by the inter-religious organizations of CPWR and form a forum of intensive encounter, above all of continuous thematic discussion. In Chicago the Assembly passed the Declaration Toward a Global Ethic, and at the Parliament in Cape Town, too, the Assembly was to be given a central role, that of adopting the document presented by CPWR, entitled 'A Call to Our Guiding Institutions'.

This document was drafted in a three-year process of redaction and consultation; around five hundred figures from all religions were involved in the discussion. From the beginning it was understood as a direct continuation of the Chicago Global Ethic Declaration, a next step in the global ethic process. A programmatic statement at an early stage of the preparation stated: 'The Declaration Toward a Global Ethic and the proposed Call to Our Guiding Institutions will form the basis for the main work of the 1999 Parliament Assembly. The abstract principles of the Global Ethic can find concrete expression in specific calls to government, business, education, the media and religion.'

However, the Call and the process of working it out also gave a specific impetus to the whole concept of the Parliament in terms of content; here the phrase 'gifts of service to the world' plays a central role. The essential dynamic of the Cape Town Parliament was provided by the motivation of religious and spiritual groups, associations, organizations and individuals to follow the Call of CPWR to offer and stimulate specific programmes, activities and enterprises, both material and spiritual services, which were to be concrete signals for a better world on the threshold of the new millennium. Such gifts could consist in the joint social action of a group for the handicapped in society or equally in the regular personal prayer or meditation of an individual. The dynamic of giving, of unselfish and generous giving, is here regarded as a specific expression of practical spirituality and thus as a central contribution of religious and spiritual individuals and groups in particular. In this 'millennium dynamic' the gifts of the world are now themselves regarded as examples of the 'creative collaboration' of religions and social institutions that is being called for. So the document is meant also to call on these institutions to perform such specific services for society and the world in the interest of a shared future.

The Cape Town Parliament and the dynamic it addresses cannot be assessed adequately without the heavily symbolic impact of the change of millennia, the 'millenium moment'. In the end the date of December 1999 was no more a coincidence than the collaboration between CPWR and the Millennium Institute in Washington, DC over the Parliament.

After reading the first draft in September 1998, the Global Ethic Foundation under the presidency of Hans Küng felt that it in particular was called on to make substantive proposals for improving the text, though its judgment on the document was in principle positive. After all, the text built strongly on the theme of a global ethic and claimed to be developing it. In intensive detailed work the Foundation compiled an improved draft which largely took over the structure of the previous text but expanded it and deepened it considerably in both content and extent.

III. Cape Town 1999: creative engagement in the service of our common world

1. The Parliament as an overall event

The Third Parliament of the World's Religions was held at different locations in Cape Town from 1–8 December 1999. In all, more than 7,000 people from more than 75 countries took part in it, averaging between 4,000 and 5,000 every day. Two things in particular stood out about the event:

• The experience of religious, spiritual and cultural diversity, encounter, exchange and inspiration;
• Grappling with the decisive problems (critical issues) of our world and seeking the ethical convergences which make common involvement and action possible.

In a similar way to the German *Kirchentag* in the Christian sphere, the Parliament thus offered a mixture of existential-emotional and reflective-committed moments. Here it became clear from the scheme that it was not concerned to create a new religion or to diminish the valuable uniqueness of each individual religious or spiritual way. The participants showed that the religions and spiritual movements can encounter one another in a spirit of respect, dialogue and collaboration and together look for ways of facing the challenges of the new century. The microcosm of the new South Africa in upheaval was an appropriate place for making people aware of this, and 'Embracing South Africa' was also one of the five themes of the Parliament. A variety of occasions, symposia and cultural events made the host country constantly present under various aspects, not least in the very welcome appearance of Nelson Mandela at the Parliament.

The other four blocks of themes at the Parliament were:

• Religion and spirituality meet;
• come into contact with one another;
• call for creative engagement;
• bring gifts of service.

Participants could join in and help to shape more than 860 elements in the programme. In general the programmes could be put into three categories: the question of religious, spiritual and cultural identity; ways of inter-religious dialogue; and the decisive problems of our time. Working groups and seminars on particular themes, symposia lasting several days, cultural activities and offerings, prayer, worship, meditations by the individual religions and also inter-religious celebrations – the wealth of offerings led to CPWR being called on from different sides to reduce the programme considerably at future Parliaments.

A central and motivating dimension of the Parliament was the project 'Gifts of Service to the World'. Starting from the conviction that the members of the religions must perceive their responsibility for the future of the world in a quite specific way, in the two years before the Parliament CPWR had prompted individuals, groups and organizations to produce projects which were to diminish suffering, further co-existence in harmony, and help to build up a better world. 300–400 such projects were described in a 'Book of Gifts' which was handed to participants in Cape Town as they registered. During the Parliament a great many other projects were suggested. The role of the Parliament Assembly, which met on the last three days of the Parliament, from 6–8 December in Cape Town Civic Centre, must be seen in connection with this dynamic of the 'Gifts of Service'.

2. The Parliament Assembly

More than 350 persons, leading religious and spiritual figures, scholars and activists, formed the core of the Parliament Assembly. In addition there were around a hundred 'participating observers' who represented different social institutions from outside the religions: government, science, education, art and media, science and medicine, international inter-governmental organizations and organizations of civil society. This composition reflected the main task of the Assembly, namely to reflect on the possibility of 'creative engagement' between the religions and the guiding institutions, on the basis of the 'Call to our Guiding Institutions' in respect of the decisive problems facing our time. Work was done in group sessions with the aim of thinking out and describing specific projects and actions to be implemented all over the world in coming years. The dynamic of the process and its real goal is expressed in the themes of the four subsequent sessions: religious and spiritual perspectives relating to the Call which are to lead the guiding institutions to collaborate and address the decisive problems, projects of hope and service. At the end of the meeting, more than 200 ideas for new projects had been proposed.

So the Parliament Assembly was not a deliberative or legislative assembly for delegates, a platform for speeches, resolutions or politic action. Rather, it offered a forum for the participants in which they could get together in interaction and dialogue and thus set the process of creative engagement in

motion. In this sense the Call to our Guiding Institutions was also the turning point and hinge of the Assembly, though it was not discussed further –
after all, it had come into being in a process of consultation and redaction
extending over three years and producing four drafts, in which more than
500 people had given their advice. The Call served as a guideline for the
Assembly; the emphasis was to lie on the process that had been stimulated,
not on the document. In this sense the CPWR, too, sees its task for the three
years after Cape Town as being primarily that of co-ordinating and support-
ing the hundreds of projects as 'Gifts of Service'. First the projects are to be
put into categories; similar projects are to be brought together and synergies
produced which will network the different initiators and supporters. The
next meeting point will be the fourth Parliament of the World's Religions,
which is planned for 2005.

Nevertheless, for all the desirable orientation on praxis, the most tangible
result of the Third Parliament of the World's Religions will remain this
document, just as the 1993 Chicago Parliament is closely identified in
public with the Declaration Toward a Global Ethic. So I shall now go on to
give some extracts from the Call by way of example and comment on them,
selecting those which are of particular relevance in the context of globalization. The complete English text is available on the Internet.[5]

IV. A Call to Our Guiding Institutions

1. Character and function of the Call

> *A Call to Our Guiding Institutions* is not a prescriptive or admonitory
> document. It is instead an appeal for active, ongoing dialogue about the
> creation of a just, peaceful, and sustainable future on behalf of the entire
> Earth community. For this reason, the Call consists of specific, particular
> invitations rather than sweeping declarations or hectoring injunctions.
> Furthermore, the authority of the Call will come only in small measure
> from its endorsement by religious and spiritual leaders. Its strength flows
> primarily from its expression of beliefs and convictions already deeply
> held – and held in common – by the world's religious and spiritual com-
> munities, and from the collaborations each part of the Call may inspire.

Thus the introduction to the document.

It is about making the global ethic concrete with the insight that the world
is essentially shaped by a set of influential institutions with which there
needs to be 'creative engagement'. Such engagement can guarantee the
ethical foundations of institutional action and thus make a contribution

towards a 'just, peaceful and sustainable world'. That is the main aim of these efforts, described in a terminology which recalls the Conciliar Process of the Christian churches in the 1980s and 1990s entitled 'Justice, Peace and the Integrity of Creation'; here the 'preservation of creation' is expressed by the term 'sustainability', which culturally is more widely accepted and is widespread today; in particular it has the life of future generations in view. The Call is thus addressed to all people in so far as we are all members or collaborators in one or more of the institutions addressed; thus what is meant is not 'the others' on whom people with a religious and spiritual commitment would have to make demands. That is simply because 'religion' is itself one of the institutions addressed; here, however, at some points it is described as a separate dimension which is to collaborate with all the other institutions.

2. *The structure and composition of the Call*

First of all, under the heading 'From the Global Ethic to the Call to our Guiding Institutions' a number of introductory texts have been inserted. The number of them seems disproportionate, and many passages in them seem repetitive. In the first chapter, 'Introduction', the clear statement that the Call represents a next step in the application of the principles of the global ethic is important, as is the explanation quoted above of the nature of the Call. The content of this is once again deepened in the following chapter, 'Rationale', and the motivation for this process is explained in terms of the need to approach the visions of a better world:

> Sustained encounters between people of different religious, spiritual, and cultural traditions have heightened the momentum towards actualizing our many visions of a better world, as well as stronger possibilities for establishing ethical common ground. New awareness of shared ethical principles opens the way into a new era of creative engagement – where we find and implement new modes of outreach, co-operation, and constructive common action, not only among the world's religions but among all of the world's guiding institutions.

Extracts from the four 'directives' of the Declaration Toward a Global Ethic are repeated as an example of these shared ethical principles. In a second stage the important thing is to relate these impulses to what are in fact the burning problems of the world, to express the 'critical issues' with which creative engagement is needed: 'disintegrating community, unrelenting demand on the Earth's limited resources, aggravated injustice, growing divisions between rich and poor, spiritual indirection. At the same time, if we address these agonies from the perspective of shared moral commitments, we can find hope.'

To meet these challenges, programmatically six ways are indicated, some of which in turn are directly related to individual problem fields:

- Building unity in diversity (pluralism, dialogue);
- Commitment to sustainability (ecology);
- Striving for justice (poverty and development).

Closely connected with this are:

- Solidarity and service;
- Seeking spiritual grounding;
- Creative engagement.

At last the Call proper follows, but not immediately, since after a list of the institutions addressed there is yet another brief repetition of the motivation and purpose, and again before the Preamble there is a solemn summary of what has already taken more than fourteen pages to say; it will also be repeated once again in the Preamble which follows. However, this inflation and redundancy in the redaction and the content should not divert attention from the pioneering content of the Call to Our Guiding Institutions itself.

In the Preamble the authors and signatories put themselves in the threefold role which leads them to express their joint responsibility for the world in this form: as human beings, as religious and spiritual persons, and as members of the world community. Precisely at this last point, once again the principle of humanity, 'Every human being must be treated humanely' and the four directives of the Global Ethic Declaration are confirmed. Now follow the eight individual calls to:

- Religion and spirituality
- Government
- Agriculture, labour, industry and commerce
- Education
- Arts and communications media
- Science and medicine
- International intergovernmental organizations
- Organizations of civil society

The eight calls each have an identical structure, and as in the Global Ethic Declaration the individual structural elements are labelled A–C. Under A the vision and hope are sketched out of a world in which, and for the building of which, the institution addressed may play a positive role that furthers community and peace. Part B gives a brief description of the positive role of each institution, the challenges facing it in our world situation, and suggestions formulated more generally about the way in which it can meet these challenges. Part C forms a transition to the concrete calls or invitations, which are then numbered in Arabic, with the two following sentences which are always formulated in the same way:

> We call on the institutions of [e.g. religion and spirituality] to develop practical ways to engage creatively with other guiding institutions in pursuit of a just, peaceful, and sustainable world.
>
> In this spirit, we invite all individuals, communities, groups, and organizations engaged with the institutions of [e.g. religion and spirituality] to reassess their roles for the next century.

The close relationship to the 1993 Global Ethic Declaration is brought out by extended quotations in the margins of the text which refer directly to the particular social institution addressed.

3. A survey of select calls

(i) Religion and spirituality

In this context, the role of religion and spirituality is seen especially in its ethical contribution to world problems:

> When individuals and communities struggle with ethical questions, religion and spirituality provide necessary and trustworthy values, norms, motivations, and ideals, all grounded in an ultimate reality. At the same time, ethical challenges demand that religious and spiritual people bring their most cherished principles to bear in the real world. How should we treat the stranger in our midst? What claim do the needs of others make on our lives and energies? How should we respond to the threats of an enemy? It is in answering such questions that religious and spiritual communities live their convictions.

The attitudes of hospitality and solidarity, particularly to the needy and the oppressed, are presented as being particularly relevant.

> From such a perspective, our religious and spiritual communities can best serve by extending the hospitality that our traditions teach. In solidarity with those in need, we can act with compassion, generosity, and courage to build a just and joyous life for all.

Here a second task is emphasized: first the strengthening of mutual collaboration among the religions themselves, though, secondly, this is always in the interests of the whole of society and the world, and thus has an external effect. Basically, here the global ethic slogan 'No world peace without religious peace' is being spelt out.

Each is invited:

1. to deepen respect and mutual welcome between religious and spiritual communities – in that spirit of hospitality which is to be found in each tradition;
2. to strengthen the search for those shared ethical and spiritual values and principles that can enable religious and spiritual communities to engage creatively with one other and with the world;
3. to encourage religious and spiritual individuals and communities to speak out for the welfare of all human beings in the name of their own values and in solidarity with others;
4. to provide leadership to assure that the Earth is respected, revered, and protected;
5. to find practical means to bring those elements of their teachings that address justice, peace, and care for future generations to wider and more immediate effect through engagement with the other guiding institutions;
6. to work closely with the institutions of government to bring religious teachings and values to bear in the struggle against corruption, dishonesty, and bribery at all levels;
7. to safeguard against the use of religious and spiritual belief and practice as briefs for intolerance, tools for political manipulation, or warrants for conflict, terror and violence;
8. to urge their adherents to work together – within and across traditions – to respond directly to the critical issues facing the world: intolerance; racism; violence; the threat of annihilation through the use of nuclear weapons; social, political, and economic injustice; systematic deprivation and exploitation of children and women; and ecological degradation;
9. to promote service in solidarity and in partnership with the poor and vulnerable to the entire human family and to the Earth as an affirmation of their teachings on personal spiritual growth, social justice, and life lived in ever-deepening relationship to Ultimate Reality.

(ii) Agriculture, labour, industry and commerce

The eight concrete invitations to these institutions spell out different facets of one and the same basic demand: economic power has to be at the service of justice and the common good.

> Consequently, economic power should be wielded in the service of economic justice and the commonweal. Wealth should be used equitably. State economic plans, corporate financial investments, agricultural techniques, and industrial processes should always do justice to human dignity and the community of life on earth.

Business is not an end in itself but must be related to a diminution of poverty, the establishment of justice in trade (for example, making it possible for all peoples equally to have access to world markets), fair wages and the creation of humane conditions of work. For this, the development of common ethical standards, especially in a globalized economy, is unavoidable. The individual invitations are concerned with this. Here again the main aim of sustainability appears in the centre, for all are invited:

7. to become at once exemplars and advocates of sustainability, carefully weighing short-term economic benefits against the continued viability of the Earth's ecosystem and the constant basic needs of the whole human community.

The spirit of the whole Call, which is born of a desire for co-operation, collaboration and networking, is reflected by invitations which seek to work against the tendency of the globalized economy to pursue its own interests independently of the other social institutions:

5. to bring their collective experience, knowledge, and skills at persuasion and innovation into partnerships with organizations of civil society dedicated to the rights of working men and women, intercultural and inter-religious understanding, social justice, ecology, and community-based economics;
6. to create joint structures with other guiding institutions to address more immediately and effectively the principal problems of our time, including severe ecological degradation, the deep indebtedness of poorer countries, massive unemployment, the widely unrewarded labours of women, and generations of poverty and malnutrition.

In this context it should be noted that on the prompting of the Global Ethic Foundation, after the reading of a first draft the call to commerce was put after the call to government, so as to indicate clearly the primacy of politics over business even in the structure of the document.

(iii) International intergovernmental organizations

Life in the 'global village' calls for new models, a new paradigm of international relations. Many problems today go beyond frontiers and can no longer be approached and solved simply by the regulations of nation states. On the basis of the work which has already been done over many decades by the United Nations Organization, its ancillary organizations and other intergovernmental organizations, both regional and in sectors, more resolute steps must be taken today to further communication and collaboration between the nations and peoples.

> If these international organizations are to wield their enormous influence for the public good, they must pursue economic and social justice, support efforts at self-determination and self-sufficiency, and move the world further along towards the equitable sharing of resources. Each organization must also acknowledge, honour and act to promote a sense of the world as a single, albeit admirably diverse, community that attends patiently and comprehensively to human needs within a larger delicately balanced environment.
>
> A singular question emerges: How can citizens of the world ensure that all international intergovernmental organizations are grounded in shared ethical principles – fairness, equity, compassion, and concern for the abiding welfare of every succeeding generation?

In the concrete invitations these organizations are now in practice reminded of their responsibility and possibilities for action, from cultural exchange through the remission of debts to poor countries and the supervision of transnational concerns to migration, help in catastrophes and protection of the environment. On the one hand this is certainly justified because of the broad scopes of these organizations, but in this text it suggests the appearance of a kind of 'panacea for the salvation of the world', which is asking too much. In this particular section the Call warms up generalizations rather than really describing a new role for these organizations. In any case, most of what is said corresponds to the fields of the tasks of the intergovernmental organizations which have already been discussed.

(iv) Organizations of civil society

As is well known, this area of social life is very much on the up and up, and in particular the rise of a civil society is regarded as an important indicator in the process of democratization. What is meant by this in the formulation of the Call is 'the network of voluntary, non-governmental associations – clubs, youth groups, sports and service groups, professional organizations, trade unions, cultural alliances, independent political parties, philanthropic funds, advocacy centres, community coalitions – that provide the fertile soul in which an expansive, responsible citizenship takes root and flourishes'.

These groups make the voice of the basis of society heard; they represent its diversity of opinion and therefore also have the task of encouraging social dialogue. They too are at the service of the social good:

> Thus, the chief task of civil society is to broaden the scope of citizen participation, to mediate between the community and the state, and to deepen the pluralistic exchange of ideas. Organizations of civil society have a special responsibility to cultivate and demonstrate moral leadership if they are to contribute to the elevation of public discourse and collective action on behalf of a better world.

In a pluralistic society and world a culture of dialogue and constructive controversy is vitally necessary. That here civil society has a central task becomes clear in several of the invitations, when the important thing is:

7. to clear the public forum of all assumptions that disagreement is equivalent to treason, so that opinion and action are neither compelled nor withheld out of fear;
8. to listen to critics and consult with opponents, and to attend patiently to internal controversy, promoting the active, positive agency of each individual and group;
9. to make dialogue possible and promising where it seems most unlikely, especially among groups that consider themselves long-standing rivals for power, prestige, or pride of place;
10. to help establish new templates of interaction and participation as they expand their partnerships with national governments and international agencies, so that co-operative, inclusive, and non-adversarial approaches to decision-making become the norm at every level of society.

The Call to our Guiding Institutions concludes with an Endorsement which all the signatories are said to subscribe to and which, like the Global Ethic Declaration, ends with a commitment:

> As persons reflecting the broad diversity of the Earth's religious, spirit-ual, cultural, ethnic and racial communities,
> we the undersigned join with the Council for a Parliament of the World's Religions in issuing this Call to our Guiding Institutions.
> We embrace the spirit of this document.
> We applaud its invitation to creative engagement.
> We commit ourselves to the realization of its aims.
> We seek to serve as role models and examples within the institutions with-in which we are engaged.
> We urge all thoughtful and concerned persons to join with us.

Both the Declarations of the Parliaments of the World Religions, in Chicago in 1993 and Cape Town in 1999, are moral appeals and not legal texts or simplistic instructions for individual and social life in a complex world. This is expressed even more clearly in Cape Town in the title 'Call'. The documents seek to give impetus to the search for common foundations in our world, which is one yet at the same time split between globalization and fragmentation. The scarlet thread of the Cape Town Call lies in two terms, the realization of which is seen as necessary for a peaceful, just and sustainable world: 'creative engagement' and 'service'.

In a world which is increasingly becoming a network, co-operative approaches must stand in the foreground. The world system of the Cold War built on confrontation has certainly given place to new confrontations, but today nevertheless there is the opportunity for a co-operative model of international relations, provided that leaders new and old do not see the implementation of their main interests as the chief goal of politics. In this context the Cape Town Call has a due place, given that the goal that it strives for is the creative engagement of all social institutions rather than confronta-tion and constant rivalry. It is to be hoped that religion is in a position to fulfil its role as one of many social forces in an open discourse and dialogue and creatively to share in opening up new ways instead of nostalgically long-ing for its old domination.

Ultimately, for all institutions involved, the important thing is service, not domination. Beyond doubt every group and every individual may have its own interests which it rightly pursues. But in a co-operative world the pursuit of particular interests should not distract attention from the wider contexts. That is true in the present, e.g. in respect of the blatant injustices and inequalities between poor and rich, which seem to be getting even greater; and it will also be true in the future, in respect of the opportunities for the life of future generations in an endangered environment. Here the watchword is sustainability.

Now for some years it has been possible to set up initiatives in which religions or organizations with an ethical orientation have made new efforts at such creative engagement with other social agents and vice versa. One international example is the World Faiths Development Dialogue, a high-ranking working group involving representatives of the religions and the World Bank in the service of humane development. The Global Ethic Foundation is also taking steps in this collaboration on the basis of the idea of a global ethic. The interplay of a global ethic with politics, business, education and the different branches of science has found a basis for reflection in two books, *A Global Ethic for Global Politics and Economics* and *Wissenschaft und Weltethos (*Science and Global Ethic).[6] The Global Ethic Foundation has also been working for this co-operation at a quite practical level, most recently in a joint symposium on ethical questions with top managers from transnational businesses (March 2001 in Baden-Baden) and in its many everyday activities with teachers and in adult education.

However, the religions must also be on their guard against allowing themselves to be exploited in their collaboration with powerful partners and then unintentionally serving the interests of the latter rather than the common good. It is not enough if, for example, when political institutions or businesses have some ethicists or even theologians, this only serves to cultivate their image or even to hang an ethical cloak over their usual practices. Even in a networked world, a collaboration of the religions with other social institutions can in the long term be creative and a real service to a more humane world only if it also contains aspects of critical detachment and prophetic challenge over against the 'powers and authorities'.

Translated by John Bowden

Notes

1. Marcus Braybrooke, *Faith and Interfaith in a Global Age*, Grand Rapids and Oxford 1998. See above all the chapters 'The Declaration Toward a Global Ethic' (pp.73–88) and 'New Developments and a New Agenda' (pp.89–102).
2. Günther Gebhardt, *Zum Frieden bewegen. Friedenserziehung in religiösen Friedensbewegungen*, Hamburg 1994. See above all the section on 'The World Conference of the Religions for Peace' (pp.86–8).
3. See also Hans Küng and Karl-Josef Kuschel, *A Global Ethic. The Declaration of the Parliament of the World's Religions*, London 1993.

4. William Swing, *The Coming United Religions*, San Francisco 1998; see above all the chapter 'Do We Have the Courage to Create a Global Ethics?' (pp.39–52).
5. At http://www.cpwr.org.
6. Hans Küng, *A Global Ethic for Global Politics and Economics*, London 1997; Hans Küng and Karl-Josef Kuschel, *Wissenschaft und Weltethos*, Munich and Zurich 1998.

II. Achieving Universal Values:
Theological Reflections

Compassion as a Global Programme
for Christianity

HILLE HAKER

Introduction: dangerous memory

'Compassion as a global programme for Christianity?'[1] That sounds provocative, and not only for the global ethic programme, which insists on a
minimal consensus on values, criteria and basic attitudes that transcends
cultures.[2] It sounds even more provocative for the current political tendency
at the beginning of the twenty-first century – a tendency which Johann
Baptist Metz has cuttingly labelled 'cultural amnesia'.

Compassion as a global programme for Christianity as Metz understands
it claims to be a universal programme at least for the religions, but in fact for
humanity generally. So there is no retreat into the particular niche of the
religious confession, which the liberalistic, compliant, amnetic culture of the
religions all too readily points to. There is no communitarian relativistic
programme which hurts no one and therefore can change nothing. To this
degree Metz sees himself linked to his counterpart within theology, the
global ethic programme. But unlike Küng's catalogue of values and responsibilities, compassion cannot even build on a minimal ethical consensus
which makes individual virtues a responsibility, in so doing possibly under-
mining the notion of freedom and stamping the memory of the sufferers on
all too tiny coins.[3]

In view of the globalization which goes with a 'constitutional pluralism',
the question arises, as Metz puts it, 'how a theology "with the face of the

world" . . . goes on the offensive against this pluralism without evading the questions of truth and authority and without abandoning the conviction that Christianity also has something to say to all human beings precisely because of this constitutional pluralism'.[4] Accordingly, theology understood in universalistic terms must stand in the tradition of a 'reflective monotheism', a monotheism which understands 'God's passion as compassion', in other words 'as the compassion springing from God's passion, as a participatory perception of the suffering of the other, as active remembrance of the suffering of the other'.[5] This monotheism, with its concept of the unity of the love of God and neighbour, is in some sense a rival to a mysticism of suffering which is apolitical in the sense that it dissolves the relationship of mysticism and morality in favour of mysticism.

Thought of as a political programme, compassion is the first element of a peace policy which allows the suffering of the other, the partner in the conflict, to stand alongside one's own suffering, which perceives it and integrates it into historical memory. Secondly, the notion of compassion can inspire a new politics of recognition, in so far as it sets the asymmetrical recognition of treaty partners alongside the symmetrical recognition. According to Metz this does not imply any emphatic concept of politics, but it does imply the necessary association of morality and politics. But thirdly, compassion may set cultural and political memory over against cultural amnesia, a memory which 'cries out for justice' and is opposed to political and cultural forgetfulness.

The universalism of compassion is based on the universality of suffering. Rightly understood, reason subjects itself to the 'authority of the sufferers', whose universalistic 'claim to validity' must be perceived and acknowledged. Reason, ethics and theology or the church, along with religions and cultures, cannot ignore this claim to the perception of the suffering of sufferers and the emotional and political recognition of their right – they can only submit to it. But is not the aim here the same as that of the 'consensus programme' in the global ethic? No, says Metz, for 'a global ethic is not a consensus product. Anyone who wants to derive this global ethic from assent alone forgets that the consensus, the assent, of all can be the consequence of a universal claim but not its basis and criterion.'[6]

Compassion is empathy, but also God's gracious concern for human beings and that of human beings for one another. Compassion is not a sophisticated concept of the Christian tradition but carries within itself a 'dangerous memory' if one investigates its semantic history more closely. For compassion is also remembrance of God's care in the exodus experience, belief in the resurrection of Christ and the hope for redemption. Thought of in exclusively individualistic terms, the political dynamite of Christian faith would turn into bourgeois contentment or allow itself to be reduced to a postmodern future performance. With the memory of God's mercy the notion of compassion at the same time provokes the only appropriate human answer to human suffering.[7] Compassion is compassion towards the sufferers and participation in their suffering and as such is a central element of love of neighbour. Metz is concerned with this ethical dimension, and that will be my concern here.

I. The theology of Johann Baptist Metz

1. Anamnetic reason

Metz's main attention is focussed on the appropriateness of talk of God, which can be thought of legitimately only in connection with talk and action of and with human beings. I want simply to mention four key theological terms which underlie the programme of compassion.

First of all comes the key term *anamnetic reason*. It is more than the complement to a 'pure' reason which is at core ahistorical. Anamnetic reason is also not only, as Habermas thinks, the 'invasion of philosophy (or theology) by historical thought'.[8] It is rather that 'dangerous memory' which in the Hebrew *zkr* combines memory with ethical impulse: 'Israel, remember your God who brought you up out of Egypt – remember your God who thought of you in Egypt.' Metz's concept of anamnetic reason, which he owes first of all to Walter Benjamin, is equally an ethical concept, and thus also at the same time a prophetic–political concept. With it Metz takes the field against 'cultural amnesia', against the forgetting of the specific memory which today still in Germany is above all memory of the victims and perpetrators of Auschwitz, and he takes the field against forgetting the memory itself, which has found a place deep in our culture.

Not only Judaism, but Christianity, too, is established on this principle of memory – the farewell discourses in the Gospel of John and the memorial meal itself point a clear way here. Anamnetic reason makes itself concrete in the memory of God in so far as this also expresses the memory of human suffering. 'To speak of this God means to express the suffering of others and to lament responsibility neglected and solidarity refused.'[9] Moreover it becomes concrete in the memory of Christ as the *memoria passionis* [the memory of his suffering]. We could say that compassion is an ethical implication of the anamnetic conception of reason understood theologically – compassion, allowing oneself to be affected by the suffering of others, makes the memory dangerous because and in that it looks the sufferers themselves in the eyes. As Psalm 22 also says of God: 'He does not hide his face from him, he has heard his cry.'[10] A further aspect seems to me important in the emphasis on a theology of memory, but now understood in the narrower sense of memory: memory is the mode of narrative, as is emphasized by all theories of narrative since Aristotle's *Poetics*. But now narrative is the medium of religious experience, remote from any romantic immediacy of the experience of God, which moreover here loses its identity as being in principle other. Rather, religious experience includes the reflective memory of the exodus narrative, the judgment, the repentance, the hope for redemption after the resurrection narrative, in short the memory of the history of God's covenant with his people and finally with all peoples, meant in the two senses of the word. So in respect of religious experiences, too, in the sense of the Jewish-Christian religion it is dangerous memory.[11]

2. Negative universalism

The second key term that I want to mention is *negative universalism*, as the opposite to a universalism of domination. A universalism of domination at least implicitly imposes its own values on all possible cultures, but in contrast to imperialism does not have recourse to power and strength but to the 'nature' of human beings or anthropological assumptions. Like Küng, Metz too is sceptical here: he takes the critique of various theoreticians of culture seriously, but on the basis of anamnetic reason formulates the universality of suffering as a universal evil as the starting point of ethical and cultural understanding,. This divided negative as a universal basis for understanding between cultures, as opposed to a minimal consensus of positive values, produces a strong motivation for universal responsibility and, Metz thinks, an obedience which precedes any moral foundation:

> Our 'neighbour' and thus partner in our responsibility is never just the one whom we regard and allow as such. The sphere of responsibility, the extent of this responsibility, is in principle unlimited. The criterion for its measure and extent is and remains the suffering of others, like the man who fell among robbers in Jesus' story, whom the priest and levite pass by 'out of higher interests'.[12]

For Jon Sobrino, the most massive form of suffering today is suffering from poverty, violence and structural injustice which slowly and violently leads to death. According to Metz, in language taken from Nelly Sachs, this poverty, but also reflection on Auschwitz, is a 'landscape of screams', and this experience is the experience underlying compassion.[13]

But theology goes beyond the question of appropriate action in the face of the universality of suffering and thus the ethical question of how to deal with suffering. Theodicy raises the question of God – it begs for deliverance as Israel begs for deliverance, as Jesus calls on his God, and as all sufferers literally beg for deliverance somewhere. Theodicy is the perception of the suffering of others, the cry of theology for deliverance, a lament which does not know whether it will be heard, how it can ever be heard. And thus, as Ottmar Fuchs rightly says, it also becomes complaint against God, accusation. Care is one side of compassion as a response to the despair of sufferers. But the compassionate cry for justice is the other.

3. Limited time and orthopraxy

In view of this radicalization of the question of God as a question *to* God, my third key term is that according to Metz theology is always also eschatology, with a strong apocalyptic colouring. As Walter Benjamin has it, it is the expectation of the messianic time. Eschatological theology, as *theology of the 'limited time'*, to use Metz's words, expects, more impatiently than patiently in view of the suffering of specific individuals, a break in history, a break between the present and history which is a history of injustice and suffering.[14]

The fourth key term takes me back to the starting point, anamnetic reason. According to Metz, the justification of faith does not take place by means of a theoretical proof of God but is the *orthopraxy* [right action] which is the foundation of faith. Here again Metz knows that he is at one with the theology of liberation:

> In the face of a suffering world, one's primary reaction is that of a compassion intent on eliminating such suffering. Like any other human and Christian activity, theology participates in this primary reaction, though in its own specific way. Thus theology will become an *intellectus amoris*, which will include the historical specifications that love assumes when confronted with a suffering people (love as justice) . . . In contemporary terminology, compassion becomes liberation. I am thus affirming that there is something ultimate, pre-theological and even pre-religious in such compassion, just as there is in the suffering of today's world.[15]

Along the lines which govern liberation theology, orthopraxy in the sense of a theology of memory of the suffering of others means the quest for justice, a justice which is grounded in compassion. This specific compassion is not a compassion from above, but means the literal recognition of the other, who is not only the universal vulnerable human being but the concrete human being, who encounters people hurt, humiliated, robbed of their happiness.

The whole of Metz's theology underlies these few key terms. But it also contains a question to the ethical approaches which are currently dominant, in so far as these start from an exclusively egalitarian universalism, and it implies a critique of any ethics which seeks to resolve conflicts of interests by morally legitimated processes (procedural approaches).

But is the idea of compassion also as programmatic, as fundamental to ethics as Metz nevertheless suggests? Or on closer inspection does the ethical impulse which stems from it dissolve into a mere appeal for good will? Is there a correlation between compassion with a theological orientation and the ethic of compassion known to the ethical tradition? And can theological ethics make an independent contribution towards the mediating of theological and ethical understanding? So the theme of my second part is the question in what way empathy, or, more usually compassion, is expressed in ethical reflection.

II. Compassion and empathy in ethics

1. The origin and value of empathy

Two sets of themes characterize the historical discussion of the concept of empathy. First there is the dispute over the *origin* of compassion: is this feeling innate and thus part of the human make up, is compassion a passive affect and to be determined largely independently of rationality, or is it first evoked by upbringing and thus an acquired virtue? No final verdict has been passed, but ethicists today are agreed that compassion or empathy can at any rate be dependent on upbringing and education. Despite all the criticism of the Enlightenment theatre of Lessing and Schiller, this was and still is the approach by means of aesthetics and ethics today, for example in Martha Nussbaum.

Secondly, however, the history of the ethical discussion of compassion amounts to a dispute on the *value and status* of compassion: independently of their views of the basis for the sense of compassion, the English moral-sense school, Rousseau, Lessing and especially the Romantics down to Schopenhauer see it as the virtue which makes it possible for human beings to overcome their isolation and egotism. The defenders of an ethic of compassion say that compassion is an altruistic attitude in which morality is ultimately grounded.[16]

Wide of the mark, Nietzsche said mockingly, with reference above all to the great tradition of the opponents of compassion in the Stoa, that compassion is the expression of the greatest weakness of all in human beings, ultimately based on self-interest – out of delight at the gratitude of the victim or the approval of those around, also based on delight in suffering and ultimately on fear – fear of one's own suffering and, in the history of evolution, fear of the threat from others whose movements, including changes of disposition, need to be studied so as to provide self-protection.[17]

The Stoics had already emphasized that compassion is blind, particular, subject to chance; it is the 'defect of a petty spirit which collapses at the sight of the suffering of others', as Seneca says. It is a deep conviction of Western moral philosophy that compassion is unworthy of a rational person (meaning of course a man) and Hobbes still accepts this tradition: compassion is a *perturbatio animi*, a confusion of the spirit.

These objections to compassion can be robbed of their force, since in the end they rest on far too narrow a view of reason and feelings, as we shall see; moreover, as Scheler has shown, they remain too rooted in a conception which sees compassion grounded in a reference back to oneself – like the moral impulse in the Golden Rule.[18] Nevertheless, the objections can help to develop a conception of ethics which can integrate compassion appropriately. Thus for example mediaeval theology gives compassion a specific function within ethics. For Thomas Aquinas, for instance, compassion becomes a virtue in so far as it converges with justice; in other words, justice is the criterion for the appropriateness of compassion. Here, however, the contribution of compassion is underestimated since, as I shall demonstrate, compassion is itself the expression of a comprehensive sense of justice.[19]

But another charge made by Nietzsche against the ethic of compassion hits the mark: compassion, he says, is not only self-interested and a product of the weak spirit, but in addition also knows no respect for the other. In other words, in some circumstances does not compassion extend the suffering of the other by regarding it as a condition from outside? How do we know, for example, whether a blind and deaf person is suffering and accordingly needs our compassion? How can we think of compassion and respect at the same time? How can we separate contempt from compassion?

It has to be conceded that the ethic of compassion has long failed to find an adequate answer to this charge. Among other reasons, this is because it has neglected to give an appropriate definition of the status of compassion and feelings in relation to respect for others. It has been too concerned to warn against a rationalistic moral theory – often enough misunderstood – to want to see the limits of the ethics of feeling. If one defines the status of compassion in the mode of a moral principle, one misses its specific function for morality. But if, like Kant, one pushes the feelings right to the periphery of moral reflection, one similarly misses their function. So one can say that the discussion at the beginning of modern ethics does not lead to an adequate understanding of the relationship between compassion and respect. That is the historical situation.

Now since in the current formation of theories the ethics of virtue is undergoing a renaissance which could not have been foreseen even twenty years ago, the ethic of compassion is also reviving. The ethic of compassion is so to speak sailing in the wake of the ethic of virtue. Now if this is the case, and if the mistakes of the controversy in the eighteenth and nineteenth centuries are to be avoided, then it is of central importance to clarify again the content and status of compassion or empathy within ethics. So my concern now is to develop a concept which can do justice to the demands of an altruistic understanding of compassion.

2. Shared humanity

To do this I shall take up a characteristic mentioned in an article by Lawrence Blum and attempt to deepen it – in respect of the envisaged mediation of theological-ethical and moral-philosophical reflection.[20] Blum defines compassion primarily in terms of its object. It relates to human beings, but largely also to animals and other entities which we shall not be concerned with here. The attention, the focus of compassion, is not the person as such but the state in which the person is. In order to arouse empathy, this state must be in close relation to the actual life or at least to the elementary well-being of the person; it must be capable of being described as misery, distress, suffering or the like. Thus empathy relates to a negative condition which points to a serious deficiency in respect of human life that can be described independently of subjective feeling.

Blum defines the attitude of empathy with the aid of four constitutive elements. The first constitutive element of empathy is *identification with the sufferer*. Preserving the distance but recognizing a basic similarity between it and the sufferer, the empathizing person perceives this situation, transfers it imaginatively to his or her own situation, and thus achieves the change of perspective inherent in all moral action.

The second constitutive element is *concern for the well-being of the other*.

This element ensures that the empathy is really focussed on the other and not on my notion of his or her situation. The imagination is in a way controlled and guided by concern for the well-being *of* the other, and not *for* the other, with all the paternalistic connotations of that. Compassion thus become reflective, and only in this way fulfils the condition of a moral feeling as a second-order feeling, which relates to the well-being of another. It is thus marked out as a partial concept of the more universal concept. We can also take up the third element mentioned by Blum and think about it further: Blum speaks of a '*shared humanity*' which produces compassion. Put in more general terms, empathy necessitates the conviction that there is a binding link between me and the sufferer, so that the suffering of the other meets and affects me in my person. Frequently the binding link only becomes visible through an imagined change of perspective or through attention which brings the sufferer near. In ethics, recourse is frequently had to a shared capacity for suffering rather than shared humanity as the common element. I cannot clarify this here, but it is certainly the case that, as I have already said with reference to Metz, in compassion we begin from a shared concept of the common evil, which produces a fundamental fellowship and equality in relation to the respect due, and thus transcends the *de facto* inequality between the one who suffers and the one who does not.

If we speak of empathy, we are also speaking of convictions which go with the sensitivity involved. We are also saying that these convictions, which cannot be detached from feelings but are interwoven with them, are of central importance for personal identity. In Charles Taylor's terminology, they are therefore strong valuations. This almost automatically gives rise to the fourth constitutive element of empathy mentioned by Blum, namely *duration and intensity*. A feeling which is based on convictions of central relevance cannot be completely abrupt and immediate. Thus duration and intensity are good criteria for the seriousness of a feeling. It need only be mentioned in passing that duration and intensity can suffer as a result of the modern media. It is not the attitude itself but the 'objects', the persons whose suffering we attempt to empathize with, that change so quickly that the quality of experience in compassion threatens to become shallow. Thus the greater nearness to the sufferers which is produced in the course of 'globalization' cannot lead to a blunting of the sense which is the reflex action when too much is asked of them.

We can now understand the spontaneous and reflective attitude of empathy more precisely as an attitude of perception, concerned attention and identification achieved in an imaginative way towards someone whose physical or psychological integrity is threatened, concern for the well-being of the other and the realization of a fundamental commonality which creates fellowship. Who would not recognize here the goodness which the Old and New Testament define as the ethical content of compassion, and in addition, in the concept of mercy, as a property of God which as such is reflected on in the theology of memory?[21] But in that case cannot the biblical tradition also be a medium of the specific religious and ethical experience of responsibility and concern, a reflective experience which emphasizes the central significance of compassion for action and also for faith? If empathy at least in part rests on a 'strong valuation', a conviction about the good which another lacks, then wherever possible it leads to an action which involves concern and resistance against this lack. Believers know that they are reinforced in this ethical attitude by a religious experience which is the historically mediated experience of the saving action of God, at least of his justice and mercy. The religious experience adds nothing to the ethical experience as such, but for the identity of the person who accepts this experience it is a conviction which then becomes inseparable from the ethical experience.

However, not only the content of the concept of compassion but also its normative status must be clarified. In essence, the question here is whether compassion itself is normative or whether it is an addition to what is normally called for. Our conceptual analysis has indicated that compassion and empathy are an altruistic feeling, a feeling which reacts to the suffering of another person with a desire for his or her well-being. This feeling is backed by the conviction that the state of a suffering person or a suffering collective must if at all possible be remedied. Because and in so far as compassion builds a bridge between me and the other, and also between my identity and what should be, compassion may mediate between what one wills and what should be.[22] Compassion is therefore a central ingredient of a person's moral identity; indeed I would go so far as to say that in this mediating function it is indispensable for morality. For the moral principles of respect and taking heed of persons have the same goal as compassion. In other words, the cognitive content of compassion converges with the normative demand and from the perspective of the compassionate is to be regarded as a normative demand. However spontaneous empathy may seem to be, it is therefore one of the most important sources, perhaps the most important source, of the insight why there are normative obligations for me and why I should act morally at all. Moreover, in so far as the bad state of a sufferer can be improved by action, empathy is also a motivation towards action on behalf of the other,[23] in close conjunction with the insight, which is and can be grounded in a normative way, that the sufferer has a right to this action. Thus in fact it is the case that here the verdict of reason and the verdict of feeling meet.[24] But because empathy has not only a reflective but also a 'spontaneous' side which is given an emotional label through the suffering of another, both modes of judgment have the function of controlling each other: reason controls universal justice, feeling its specific form.

However, empathy is not restricted, like normative morality, to the level of action but also continues to keep on guard where violations and integrities cannot either rest on human action or be removed by action. There can be and is empathy precisely when action comes up against its limits. Empathy may have to tread a tightrope in giving others their due in their suffering. But that tightrope indicates all the more the need for a reflective treatment of empathy.

3. Contempt of the other?

But does this conception really stand up to the charge of contempt of the other? I think that it does. For, first, the imagination of the change of perspective is not thought of naively as empathy or paternalistic identification, but must maintain a distance. Secondly, the other must himself or herself give the guidelines for determining the well-being on which the compassion is focussed. Thirdly, the reference to a common 'shared humanity' is a criterion which safeguards the preservation of the respect that is based on the normative equality of all. However, the closer definition of this sharing leaves much scope and is therefore also prone to paternalistic and ideological definitions. That makes it all the more important to link empathy up with a theory of rights which forms a basis for the normative claims of others and which for example also attempts to qualify the question of those addressed, the extent of the responsibility, the calculation of benefits and the right balance between different benefits.

With the normative theory of rights we transcend the personal relations in which empathy has its roots and without which it cannot become effective. The question now is whether empathy can be made fruitful for a theory of justice, and if so, to what extent. I want at least to mention two points which can give us a direction. The basis of justice is the universal equality of moral subjects, which is set down in the convergence of rights and responsibilities. Justice perceives the other in the mode of normative equality understood in this way, and thus as the 'generalized other'.[25] But in order to be able to take account of the individual and social inequality which is in fact to be perceived, and in order to be able to perceive persons behind the structures of injustice, the other has to be regarded as a concrete other.[26] Empathy reacts to this equality by way of a spontaneous concern which has a reflective backing. Empathy with a structural focus recognizes the asymmetry between those who suffer and those who do not, which leads to an inequality in respect of the distribution of responsibilities and rights. So here, too, the cognitive content of the verdict of the feelings coincides with the normative verdict of justice. Empathy does not transcend justice; empathy is not grace which proceeds from grace. Rather, empathy is a function, a specific dimension of justice itself; one can perhaps say that it is the 'other of justice' which itself appears in justice.

This form of justice sees that the other is special and reflects on the relevance of this special character for norms. Paradoxical though it may seem, it makes the asymmetry the starting point of the concrete recognition and respect which is called on to preserve the right praxis, including theoretical reflection on it in a theory of justice. But over and above this, empathy points to a sense of solidarity which is grounded in the benevolence of the other. To assume responsibility for the sufferer cannot therefore stop at establishing the rules of behaviour. Nor can it stop at a definition of the rights of self-defence, or make its correctness dependent on a consensus. Responsibility, which Metz's 'authority of the sufferers' recognizes as a normative point of reference, can only be formulated in a theory of justice which encounters structural injustice both individually and politically. To use a familiar image: for those lying on the ground, anyone who encounters them is infinitely far above them. Empathy which takes heed of others and recognizes their fundamental normative equality, in other words empathy appropriate to the other, strives to synchronize the movements of concern and raising up. Concern is the personal, emotional side of empathy. But 'raising up' is the practical side, the justice which produces equality where it does not exist. This is the point of the parable of the Good Samaritan, the New Testament model for the appropriate emotional empathy with the sufferer which governs action. And once again we can – and must – say that the ethical dimension of this view of ethical responsibility within a theological definition of justice can easily be communicated. That the theological concept of justice points beyond the ethical dimension to the eschatological dimension makes ethics a goad which remains until all injustice has been transformed into justice. It is not ethics but religion (the Christian religion) which gives ground for hoping that this goad is not God's last statement on suffering. However, theology must not fall in with this hope but must challenge God to a conversation; it must put the question of suffering and confront it with the 'landscape of screams', as God challenges human beings in their injustice.

Conclusion

So if compassion is to be a programme for Christianity, first a 'systematic cover' needs to be incorporated into this programme which clarifies its content and status in dialogue with the tradition of moral philosophy and moral philosophy. Here 'attentive and perceptive recognition of participation in the suffering of the other' proves to be the partial element in the more general structure of care, an attitude of concern which itself calls for training and practice.[27] It has the status of a mediating principle between what one wills and what should be. But this 'should' has to be given a basis and justified in a separate step, because involvement neither gives the basis for the moral 'should' nor can it guarantee that it is understood in universal terms. Margalit puts this sharply: 'We need morality precisely where we take no part.'[28] So if compassion is to be understood as a value programme of Christianity, then it must be understood as complementary to an ethic of human dignity which spells itself out as an ethic of human rights. This too cannot be based on a consensus nor can it issue in a procedural ethic. Nevertheless Metz puts his finger on the sore spot which Margalit identifies. Certainly morality is challenged in the face of emotional indifference. But how can indifference be overcome, if not by involvement, by compassion? And how else can moral action be motivated, if not by involvement, which also includes indignation about injustice and pain about the suffering of the sufferer?

Translated by John Bowden

Notes

1. Cf. J. B. Metz, 'Compassion. Zu einem Weltprogramm des Christentums im Zeitalter des Pluralismus der Religionen und Kulturen' in Johann Baptist Metz, Lothar Kuld and Adolf Weisbrod, *Compassion. Weltprogramm des Christentums. Soziale Verantwortung lernen*, Freiburg im Breisgau 2000, pp.9–20; id., 'Das Christentum im Pluralismus der Religionen und Kulturen', *Luzerner Universitätsreden* 14, 2001, pp.3–14.
2. H. Küng, *A Global Ethic for Global Politics and Economics*, London and New York 1997. For a discussion with the various sciences see H. Küng and K.-J. Kuschel, *Wissenschaft und Ethos*, Munich 1998.
3. The substantive problem consists above all in the fact that human rights automatically entail human responsibilities. But since the Declaration is not congruent with the United Nations Declaration on Human Rights, problems arise in respect both of the contents and also of the connection with universal human rights. For a critique of the Declaration cf. T. Hoppe, 'Weltinnenpolitik durch Weltethos? Rückfragen an das Projekt von Hans Küng', *Herder*

Korrespondenz 8, 1997, pp.410–14; id., 'Priorität der Menschenrechte', *Herder Korrespondenz* 6, 1998, pp.293–8.

4. Metz, 'Christentum' (n.1), p.3.

5. Ibid., pp.7f.

6. Ibid., p.9.

7. For more recent literature see above all S. Dybowski, *Barmherzigkeit im Neuen Testament – Ein Grundmotiv caritativen Handels*, Freiburg im Breisgau 1992; also M. Zehetbauer, *Die Polarität von Gerechtigkeit und Barmherzigkeit. Ihre Wurzeln im Alten Testament, im Frühjudentum sowie in der Botschaft Jesu. Konsequenzen für die Ethik*, Studien zur Geschichte der katholischen Moraltheologie 35, Regensburg 1999.

8. J. Habermas, 'Israel und Athen oder: Wem gehört die anamnetische Vernunft? Zur Einheit der multikulturellen Vielfalt' in Johann Baptist Metz et al., *Diagnosen zur Zeit*, Düsseldorf 1994, p.56.

9. J. B. Metz, *Zum Begriff der neuen Politischen Theologie*, Mainz 1998, pp.200f.

10. It is interesting that in his 'Ethics of Memory' Avishai Margalit also starts from a triangular relationship: 'One side of the triangle links memory with participation, the second side participation with ethics; only after that can one also localize the relationship between memory and ethics', A. Margalit, *Ethik der Erinnerung*, Max Horkheimer lectures, Frankfurt am Main 2000, p.17. And like Metz, Margalit too posits participation as the attention to the other which precedes morality.

11. Cf. e.g. J. B. Metz, *Christlicher Glaube in Geschichte und Gesellschaft*, Mainz 1977; D. Mieth, *Moral und Erfahrung I. Grundlagen einer theologisch-ethischen Hermeneutik*, Fribourg, Ch/Freiburg im Breisgau ⁴1999; id., *Moral und Erfahrung II*, Studien zur Theologischen Ethik 76, Fribourg, Ch/Freiburg im Breisgau ⁴1998.

12. J. B. Metz, 'Im Eingedenken fremden Leids. Zu einer Basiskategorie christlicher Gottesrede' in Johann Baptist Metz, Johann Reikerstofer and Jürgen Werbick, *Gottesrede*, Münster 1996, pp.3–20:12. It is not Metz but Jon Sobrino who gives this universal suffering more precise contours, contours which become the focus for ethical action: it is suffering in itself, the suffering of others, the suffering of individuals or the suffering of groups; it may be spiritual, psychological suffering or bodily, historical suffering, or a metaphysical suffering over existence. Cf. also S. Weil, *Waiting on God*, London and New York 1951.

13. J. Sobrino, 'Theology in a Suffering World: Theology as *intellectus amoris*' in Paul Knitter and Raimundo Panikkar, *Pluralism and Oppression. Theology in World Perspective*, The Annual Publication of the College Theology Society 34, Lanham 1991, pp.153–77: 155f.

14. Here Metz shows himself to be strongly influenced by Walter Benjamin's philosophy of history, which itself is in part rooted in the Jewish messianic hope and the apocalypse.

15. Sobrino, 'Theology in a Suffering World' (n.13), p.165.
16. Cf. especially A. Schopenhauer, *Über die Grundlage der Moral* (1841), Zurich edition 6, Zurich 1977; M. Scheler, *Wesen und Formen der Sympathie* (1912), Bonn 1985. W. Marx, *Ethos und Lebenswelt: Mitleidenkönnen als Mass*, Hamburg 1986, is worth investigating.
17. Cf. the polemic against the morality of compassion above all in Nietzsche's *The Dawn, Zarathustra* and *Genealogy of Morality*.
18. Cf. M. Nussbaum, 'Gefühle und Fähigkeit von Frauen' in ead., *Gerechtigkeit oder das gute Leben*, Frankfurt am Main 1999, pp.131–75; A. Leist, 'Mitleid und universelle Ethik' in Hinrich Fink-Eitel (ed), *Zur Philosophie der Gefühle*, Frankfurt am Main 1993, pp.157–87.
19. Cf. *Summa Theologiae* II/II, Qu.30.
20. L. Blum, 'Compassion' in Amelie Oksenberg Rorty, *Explaining Emotions*, Berkeley 1980, pp.507–17.
21. See S. Dybowski, *Barmherzigkeit im Neuen Testament – Ein Grundmotiv caritativen Handels*, Freiburg im Breisgau 1992; M. Zehetbauer, *Die Polarität von Gerechtigkeit und Barmherzigkeit. Ihre Wurzeln im Alten Testament, im Frühjudentum sowie in der Botschaft Jesu. Konsequenzen für die Ethik*, Studien zur Geschichte der katholischen Moraltheologie 35, Regensburg 1999; Ruth Scoralick (ed), *Das Drama der Barmherzigkeit Gottes. Studien zur biblischen Gottesrede und ihrer Wirkungsgeschichte in Judentum und Christentum*, Stuttgart 2000; B. Janowski, 'Der barmherzige Richter. Zur Einheit von Gerechtigkeit im Gottesbild des Altes Orients und des Alten Testament', ibid., pp.33–91.
22. On this point I can agree with U. Wolf, who argues in the same direction. Cf. U. Wolf, 'Haben wir moralischen Verpflichtungen gegen Tiere' in Angelika Krebs, *Naturethik: Grundtexte der gegenwärtigen tier- und ökoethischen Diskussion*, Frankfurt am Main 1997, pp.47–75; ead., 'Gefühle im Leben und in der Philosophie' in Hinrich Fink-Eitel and Bernd Lohmann, *Zur Philosophie der Gefühle*, Frankfurt am Main 1993, pp.112–35.
23. Cf. P. Stemmer, *Handeln zugunsten anderer. Eine moralphilosophische Untersuchung*, Berlin 2000.
24. 'There is no knowledge without feeling, no action without feeling, no perception without feeling, no memory without feeling – but every human feeling already either entails as feeling the moment of cognition or is at least associated with the cognition, with the aims and situations' . . . 'cognition does not stand over against emotion, but the higher forms of emotion and cognition mutually condition one another', A. Heller, *Theorie der Gefühle*, Hamburg 1980.
25. 'Justice – located on the cognitive level – is the symmetrical principle of responsibility which names the rights and responsibilities that I have towards all other persons. The other encounters me here in the role of the universalized other and shares the same responsibility which time and again is assured procedurally. Comparability, definition, calculability are characteristic of this responsibility, so all in all this is a "system of regulated, entered, codified pre-

cepts" (J. Derrida). The other level of responsibility which grows out of compassion, the affective level, is constituted by the asymmetrical principle of responsibility and is first the basis of the principle of equality. It refers to an irreplaceable individual towards whom only the I addressed has a responsibility. Incalculability, infinity, refractoriness, strangeness and heteronymity are the characteristics of this responsibility. It is what first gives rise to a moral sense.' J. Manemann, 'Kritik als zentrales Moment des Glaubens. Zur gesellschaftskritischen Dimension der Fundamentaltheologie' in Klaus Müller, *Fundamentaltheologie*, Regensburg 1998, pp.217–41: 237.

26. S. Benhabib in *Situating the Self*, 1995. Cf. also M. Nussbaum, 'Gefühle und Fähigkeiten von Frauen' in *Gerechtigkeit oder das gute Leben*, Frankfurt am Main 1999, pp.131–75. D. Sölle's concern to see an appropriate understanding of suffering which is expressed in the statement 'there is no alien suffering, there is no alien resurrection' is also to be seen against this background. See her *Suffering*, London 1975.

27. See P. Ricoeur, *Oneself as Another*, Chicago 1992.

28. A. Margalit, *Ethik der Erinnerung* (n.10), p.22.

The Challenge of Pluralism and Globalization to Ethical Reflection

FRANCIS SCHÜSSLER FIORENZA

During the last decades of the twentieth century, developments in communication technology and in the means of travel have significantly reduced the temporal and spatial distance among all parts of the globe. The remotest parts of the globe seem to be as close as a telephone call, an e-mail, or a simulcast TV news broadcast. Although world commerce at the end of the twentieth century is scarcely higher than at the beginning,[1] our situation is described as a new situation of globalization due to communications, travel, and information technologies.[2] Nevertheless, the forms of co-operation that are economic show the interdependence between the economic and communicative. Globalization should not be understood exclusively as a communication category; it also entails the exchange and interlocking of material goods within modern international capitalism. More importantly, the process of globalization involves certain ambiguities, and the intertwinement of the economic and cultural levels often leads to a commodification of the cultural as well as the material.

I. Ambiguities of globalization

The question is whether globalization means a unification or integration in any other way than the increased co-ordination of world markets and the increased efficacy of communication and travel technology.[3] How does globalization impact on (even though it may at the same time mask and hide this very impact and influence) cultural meanings, ethical norms, and religious values? This impact of globalization upon cultural and normative meanings will be explored here. The cultural impact of globalization is in my view ambivalent, if not paradoxical.

One way of interpreting the cultural phenomena of globalization is with the term 'global village'. The notion of 'world community' or the term 'global village' is very popular in some discourses. 'Global village' has a nostalgic ring and offers an attractive image. The rise of global tourism, world sports, international experience of medical crises, such as AIDS, and environmental threats from global warming, the rapid defoliation of forests and the desertification do indeed contribute to common experiences. Nevertheless, the term 'global village' is a misleading term that downplays 'cultural otherness' and economic disparities. The degree of both 'cultural diversity' and economic disparity that exists today belies the term 'global village'.

A village often has a common ethos consisting of accepted traditions, shared values, collective experiences, and communal rituals. Many parts of the world, however, are quite diverse in their cultural, ethical, and religious values. Instead of claiming that globalization produces a 'global village', one could just as equally claim that the technological advances in communication have increased our awareness of diversity and the economic advances have increased poverty and relations of dependency. We have come to recognize through increased communication and information our religious, philosophical and ethical differences. Globalization shows us that the world still consists of diverse cultures and that ethnic conflicts permeate diverse localities of the world. In our age of capitalist globalization, we can see an increased disparity between the rich and poor, not only within well-to-do countries, but also between parts of the globe.

Two tendencies move in contending directions: transnational, market and economic forces, on the one side, and increased awareness of the local values, ethnic traditions and individual preferences, on the other. This tension, moreover, is not simply a conflict between economic and cultural forces. Information and exchange technologies make possible both directions. For example, they make possible an increasingly local work because such work can be easily communicated elsewhere; a regional production easily enters an international exchange. The paradox of globalization is that globalizing tendencies are at the very same time and in the very same process both universalizing and particularizing. The result of globalization cannot be simply characterized with such terms as 'global village' or 'world community'. Globalization makes equally evident the diversity of the globe that consists of many villages with differing religious, ethical, and ethnic traditions.

Another dialectic of globalization has been well formulated by Roland Robertson's assertion that globalization is a 'twofold process of the particularization of the universal and the universalization of the particular'.[4] This dynamic comes to the fore in the ambiguous relationship the global economic networks, increasingly present in the modern economic world, have with the modern social world. In one sense the social world becomes much more uniform and commodified. There results so speak a 'McDonaldization' and commodification of culture and goods and even education. At the same time, there is powerful resistance to globalization in terms of the appeal to local traditions, the critique of religious fundamentalism,[5] and the developing understanding of the contingent significance of hybridity that is neither the deferral of identity nor the pluralist celebration of multiple identities.[6] These tensions are reflected in the questions of the pluralism of religious and ethical values and the relation of religious and ethical values to globalization.

II. Commodification as standardization and individuation

Jean Baudrillard's work on the 'consumer society' criticizes the Marxian distinction between use value and exchange value, which he alleges is based upon a fixed anthropological conception of need.[7] Instead, the consumer society has less to do with the mere passive satisfaction of existing needs than it has to do with the creation of new activities and values. The object of consumption is not simply a material good or object, but also a sign and an image. The object defines the human subject just as much as the subject defines the object. In this sense the contemporary consumer society produces a commodification that entails both human culture and human behaviour.

Commodification signifies the social development and cultural effect of capitalism upon human behaviour whereby various aspects of human activity are fragmented and objectified in relation to the market economy. This entails not simply the organization of human activity in terms of means and ends. Commodification refers to the transformation of human activity and human culture into products, objects, or commodities to be consumed. Moreover, all commodities take on within the consumer society aesthetic and evaluative dimensions. One does not simply buy a new car or a new set of clothes, but the activity associated with this. Commodification results not only in the commodification of culture, but also in the 'aestheticization' of the commodity.[8] The end result is commodification that can be understood as the integration of both the private and public realms into the logic of capitalism. In such a process not only object and commercial goods, but also aesthetic objects, cultural values, and ethical options are related to the market economy as objects of choice.

The process of commodification also indicates a certain contrast. On the one hand a correspondence exists between a market economy and liberal political virtues such as freedom of choice and individual autonomy. On the other hand, this choice and autonomy can be commodified so that what is culturally exported through the globalization of the market economy is a specifically modern Western set of cultural values. What appears as heterogeneous and offers choice is really a form of homogeneity. This dialectic between homogeneity and heterogeneity mirrors itself in ethical and religious discussions.

III. Two diverse responses

Since globalization paradoxically entails universality and unity at the same time as particularity and contingency, it raises the religious ethical issue of universality and particularity; unity and contingency. Ethical responses to the challenge of globalization display the same ambiguity and paradoxicality. The first is the advocacy of particularism and pluralism as the adequate response. This approach is represented by Richard Rorty, a leading North American pragmatic philosopher, and by Michael Walzer, a leading social ethicist; though Walzer in dealing with the issue of multinational ethics nuances his position. The other approach is represented by Karl-Otto Apel's call for a universal ethic. A final section advocates an ethic that combines valuable elements in each approach through an appeal to practical reasoning, pluralism as genuine diversity, and the notion of reflective equilibrium.

IV. Liberal choice and ethnic particularism

In dealing with the challenge of globalization, Richard Rorty underscores the effect that globalization has upon philosophical moral reasoning. Contemporary experiences of globalization make us increasingly aware of the great disparity between rich and poor, and makes us increasingly conscious of steering mechanisms that are outside the control of individual nations and states. Consequently, there is a loss of faith in the hope for global success in eliminating the inequality, as well as a loss of faith in the ability of technological and scientific advances to overcome global inequalities. Rorty sees that the result is loss of faith in cosmopolitan and universalist notions.[9]

Such a loss of faith points to the limited role of a neo-pragmatic philosophical reflection. The role is not based on its access to foundations; instead what is important is indicated by the titles of two of his most well-known articles: 'Ethics Without Principles' and 'The priority of Democracy over Philosophy'.[10] In an attack on the Kantian tradition, Rorty argues against the contrast between 'the moral point of view' and 'mere self-interest'. He disagrees with the charge that if one no longer distinguishes between morality and self-interest and if morality reflects the self-interest of those who have been similarly acculturated, then one is guilty of 'emotivism'.[11] Resisting Kant's interpretation of morality as a matter of reason, Rorty sympathizes with Hume's emphasis on sentiment. Moreover, moral progress is not a 'matter of getting closer to the True or the Good or the Right, but an increase in imaginative power'.[12] What becomes important are historical narratives with a utopian perspective that move us towards a better future rather than philosophical judgments about the good or the right. In this respect philosophy, literature, and religion are similar. The utopian, narrative, imaginative and even 'romantic' quality of religious faith serves a similar purpose to literature and philosophy.

Although Rorty seeks to challenge the commodification of modern globalization through his emphasis upon utopian imagination and through narrative histories that underscore the suffering and inequalities within our modern world, his emphasis on sentiment and preference as well as his modest claim for the superiority of Western liberal views, in that they work better, mirrors the modern market economy more than it challenges. Modern Western liberal beliefs are preferable to others because they pragmatically work better. We should for that reason seek to disseminate and increase the marketability of our ideals.

The criticism exists that some brands of European liberalism express the possessiveness and individualism of the modern economy and that the liberalism of the Enlightenment is paradigmatic for modernity.[13] Such a criticism can be brought against what some view as two differing strands of liberalism.[14] Whereas one strand advocates the autonomy of the individual, the other strand encourages diversity. The strand favouring the autonomy of the individual examines the self and social practices in relation to the autonomy of the self. The strand favouring diversity is concerned with those very differences that individuals and groups have with their distinctive notions of the good and moral life. Despite these differences, a basic similarity underlies both conceptions. Diversity and autonomy often cohere as two sides of the same coin, though one could question whether the emphasis upon autonomy undercuts the diversity and suggest that alternative understandings of both diversity and liberalism are needed. What is evident is that such an understanding of ethics that Rorty advocates fits within the parameters of individual choice that a globalized market economy presents to persons as well as to communities and nations.[15]

Less oriented on pragmatism or on individual choice and more influenced by hermeneutical considerations is Michael Walzer's attempt to develop a complex notion of justice and to apply it to international economic conditions.[16] Walzer argues in a hermeneutical fashion that ethical appeals to universal and inclusive principles often have tacit presuppositions and implicit assumptions. They often contain covert premises about human nature, the human self, and the good of society. Walzer alerts us to the interpretive or hermeneutical dimension of our conceptions of justice and our ideas about the right. Substantive principles of justice depend upon the meanings that social goods have in particular societies. Our morality and principles of justice are therefore constituted by these social meanings. These result from our existence and self-understanding as particular historical communities. Moral reasoning in this approach does not and should not abstract these thick social meanings, but should articulate their critical significance. Justice is a complex concept with specific meaning in the diverse sphere of justice.

Since ethical discourse is rooted within a specific community or traditions, attempts to apply it beyond the boundaries of communities, societies, and states separates and detaches this ethical discourse from the forms of life and thought upon which it depends. Conceptions of transnational economic justice are illusory and share the false assumption that those in differing communities with different backgrounds share basic categories and principles. The emphasis on the particular and local resists a simple application that universally covers all concrete instances. Walzer introduces the notion of 're-iterative universalism' in distinction to a 'covering law universalism', and argues for the minimalist and thin conceptions of the good for international situations.[17] There is some universalism in the recurrence of a notion in diverse societies and there are minimal conceptions, but both depend upon the thicker and complex conceptions.

V. A universal discourse ethic

A stark and paradigmatic contrast to both Richard Rorty's historicist pragmatism and Michael Walzer's interpretive ethics has been articulated by Karl-Otto Apel in his attempt to develop a universal ethic as a response to globalization. Apel argues that globalization requires a universal ethic and only such an ethic would avoid the dangers of culture-centrism and resist the surrender of self-reflective reason to historicism and relativism.[18] Apel's ethical reflections are within a deontologist and Kantian tradition. Apel's work does not stand alone. He has strongly influenced Jürgen Habermas' discourse ethic, even though it gives more emphasis to the life-world, democracy theory and institutionalization.[19] His universalist position can be compared with other diverse deontological positions that explore the universal claim entailed in ethical judgments. Ronald Dworkin,[20] Alan Gewirth[21] and the early John Rawls[22] represent in English- speaking countries this more universal approach, though they are much more sensitive to context and tradition. Otfried Höffe,[23] Reiner Wimmer[24] and to some extent Jürgen Habermas in German speaking countries seek to develop a more universalistic claim to ethics. Among theologians, Hans Küng's pleas for a world ethic would appear to belong here, though Apel sees his proposal as similar to later attempts of Walzer.[25]

Apel's proposal should be contrasted with traditional ethics, especially with regard to the foundation he proposes for his ethics. Traditionally, ethics was universal in so far as it was grounded in some metaphysical essentialist view of human nature and formulated through a specific conception of natural law. The foundation of a universal ethic either in natural law or anthropology runs up against the problem of determinacy. The historical and hermeneutical awareness of cultural diversity underscores that nature and human nature are by themselves undetermined. Different cultures and different societies interpret nature, human nature and human needs differently. Appeals to human nature, natural law and human needs as a basis for a universal have to take into account that these are by themselves insufficiently determinate and need to be further specified through historical interpretations and cultural determinations if they are to ground an ethics. If, however, they are specified through a thick description of human nature, then the universal applicability of that thick description can be challenged.[26] In contrast to this approach a discourse ethics seeks to develop a universal ethics from the very presuppositions of discourse itself. Norms such as equality, justice, mutual acknowledgment and human dignity are presuppositions in the very nature of moral discourse itself.

Apel contends that it is precisely globalization that challenges one to develop an approach differing from traditional and conventional forms of ethics. Globalization requires a universal planetary ethics. Traditional ethical traditions, which he labels micro- and meso-ethics, were based on small groups, tribes or nations. In contrast to these, a planetary ethics would be macro–ethics and would take into account the world–wide changes that result from science, technology and the international market economy. Since the rationality of science and technology is universal, this rationality challenges any ethics that appears to be local and particular. Therefore, there is a need to develop in the face of these challenges a universal ethic.

Apel consequently argues that one does not deduce such an ethic as if one were deducing moral norms from first principles or basic axioms. Instead one elaborates the transcendental pragmatic foundation of discourse ethics by reflecting on the presuppositions of argumentative moral discourses. These procedures provide only the ideal procedures for moral discourse about concrete moral problems and their resolutions. A universal ethic goes beyond the interpretive retrieval of historically and culturally contingent ethical traditions in so far as it reflects on the moral presuppositions of global moral discourse. Such an analysis should show that any discourse about ethics is committed to an impartial point of view. Apel acknowledges that such a transcendental pragmatic has not met with much acceptance among those philosophers, influenced by the more historicist, relativist and pragmatic traditions of the present.

In general, the universalist approach make an important point. The universalists, especially the Kantian, likes to criticize the particularists for the inadequacies of their approach to ethical values. They argue that the appeal to local practices and particular religious or ethical traditions tends to reflect and to support practices that might be unjust, and traditions express not so much justice as oppression and domination. Moreover, the universalists argue that the particularists do not offer an account of justice that is adequate to the globalization of the modern world. They argue that globalization entails complex economic structures and social norms that extend beyond the particular boundaries of states and nations. Therefore, an account of justice and the foundations of justice must explicate standards that have as their basis more than national standards or ethnic values. It becomes necessary to enter into conversation with those who do not share the same traditions, customs and values. They argue that the cultural particularists are blind and should search for more universal principles. However, universalism remains subject to the criticism of the particularist, that a minimalist world ethic, or a formalist discourse ethic, while claiming to be global, covertly puts forward a modern Western and European ethical perspective as universal.

VI. Practical reasoning and reflective equilbrium

The opinions surveyed above point to a mirroring of the paradoxes of globalization within ethical theories themselves.[27] An abstract formal universalism both expresses globalization and seeks to provide a universal planetary ethic. A contrasting contextual, historicist ethic argues for a grounding of morality in ethnocentric practices, customs and choices. Neither an ethnocentric or communitarian moral particularism nor a singular universal ethic can deal with the complexity of moral reflection and judgments. In the face of the ambiguities of globalization and commodification, the ethical task becomes such that one avoids having one position reflect the market ability so that ethical values are viewed primarily as ethnocentric choices whose validity depends upon their ability to work best or as an abstract formalized ethic that encompasses the global merely as a formal universalism fits all. Morality entails more than ethnocentric choice, and the possibility of a moral criticism of the particular values of a particular tribe, community, nation or civilization points to the need for a moral judgment that is based upon more than evaluative criteria that are exclusively specific to the community. Morality is more than the formal acknowledgment of the other in discourse. It both feeds upon life context and is applied to the life. The formal distinctions between the genesis and justifications of moral judgments or between the justification and application of these judgments overlook the interpretive intertwinement of both in the actual process of moral reflection. Therefore, to grasp this element, one underscores that moral rationality consists of a plurality of elements as a form of practical rationality. Moreover, there are tendencies with some representatives of each approach to flip over into the opposite position.

I have sought to develop this with reference to the notion of reflective equilibrium as it has developed in the discussions surrounding Rawls's ethical conceptions, though with different elements. Another significant approach would be Dietmar Mieth's development of combinatorial method that not only includes diverse steps within the moral judgment, but also a significant description of the phenomenology of moral experience.[28] My own suggestion seeks to develop a broad reflective equilibrium in a way that allows a plurality of moral judgments but avoids giving up the transcendent moral judgment to individual choice or to ethnic values. Some brief comments on practical rationality, background experiences and pluralism and communities of discourse will illustrate this argument.

VII. Practical rationality and ethical judgment

The analysis of practical reasoning can show how practical moral reasoning differs from the universalization of Apel and the instrumentalism of Rorty. Practical rationality displays in the exercise of moral judgments an interconnection between what is more universal and what is more particular. Moreover, an account of the diverse types of practical reasoning (from the teleological and utilitarian to action-oriented and reflective) displays practical reasoning of which Rorty's pragmatic practical rationality is only one type.[29] In practical reasoning so conceived, one does not simply go from universal principles to specific cases so that the moral reasoning consists of the application of the principle to the case through certain maxims or secondary principles. Nor is moral reasoning as a form of practical reasoning simply the reflection upon praxis as if practice by itself and in isolation could justify itself. In this regard the distinction between justification and application has a degree of validity, even if one makes choices on reasons that lack an ultimate foundation. However, the sharp distinction between justification and genesis or application (which both Habermas and Apel make) overlooks the degree to which the genesis and application of a moral judgment is part and parcel of what constitutes the judgment itself. The orientation of practical reasoning to action cannot simply be reduced to teleological judgments and to application because the genesis of a belief, its embeddedness in a life tradition, and the horizon of a tradition of ideals and practice, all contribute to the understanding of the application, justification, and meaning of a moral judgment. What goes hand in hand with practical reasoning are diverse experiences and traditions that display what is concrete and yet transcends the concrete.

VIII. Pluralism as resistance to commodification and universalization

The attempt to develop a concrete global minimalist ethic that goes beyond mere formalism or proceduralism through comparative analysis runs against the problem that concrete cultures not only have distinctive hierarchies of values, but also give certain values a different function within the totality of values. This poses a problem for all comparisons among religious belief and ethical values. For example, a comparison that acknowledges that Catholicism, Lutheranism and Judaism accord law an important place in their religious conceptions and compares their diverse concepts of law, may overlook the degree to which the Torah has such a central function in Judaism that perhaps faith, not law, might be the comparative point. Likewise within an ethical system one can point out that in one society an obligation exists to care for the poor, needy and ill out of the surplus of one's own goods, whereas in another society, the poor and the needy have basic rights to work, health, and well-being. To level these differences into a basic minimal ethic overlooks the sharp contrast between societies in which the needs of the poor are met through charity, compassion or philanthropy or legislation that seeks to guarantee basic rights to well-being.[30]

In addition, to the extent that diversity underscores a pluralism in basic values and in diverse conceptions of the good life, it points to basic objective differences in the conception of the good and virtuous life. These may be incommensurable not in the sense that their similarities and differences cannot be compared – surely one can do that – but in the sense that they cannot be measured against some universal standard or such hierarchically arranged conception of the good and the good and virtuous life.[31] The Greek hero, the Christian ascetic, Nietzschean critic, the twentieth-century analytical philosopher, the Buddhist monk, the capitalist entrepreneur and the Confucian scholar – all these incorporate diverse values and virtues that cannot be combined into a single comprehensive vision of the good. They contain values and visions of the good that starkly conflict with one another. They cannot be ranked into a single order or made to fit into a comprehensive whole. One might live these values serially in that one might change one's opinion or one's life's goals from one to another, as when a Greek hero might convert to a Christian ascetic or a modern businessman might become an ascetic monk. But they cannot be related to each other in the way of a *Bildungsroman* or of the spirit coming to consciousness of itself. Instead they stand alongside one another as alternative visions of the virtuous life. To the extent that globalization brings to consciousness such differences, to that extent it should resist any attempt to reduce these to a commodified ethic.

IX. Materiality of life and background experiences within interpretive horizons

If the above underscores difference, then there is also through the corporeality of life a certain intersecting and criss-crossing. Some material elements of experience are everywhere, for example, suffering, illness, health, aging, the environment etc. Affirming that these background material elements are everywhere is not to overlook that they are experienced only in and through different interpretation. Suffering is interpreted differently in a Christian context than it is in a Buddhist context or a humanistic context. Aging is a biological process that all human beings experience to the degree that they age. Yet it is experienced differently in a culture that respects the elderly than in a culture that has a cult of youth. Likewise, human needs and capabilities, which Martha Nussbaum highlights in her capabilities approach, are interpreted differently.[32] Even medical conceptions such as health are subject to diverse interpretation.[33] It is in relation to such aspects that cultures develop their concrete attitudes. One does not so much achieve consensus or dialogue about them, as one develops what I could call a 'criss-crossing' of judgment and attitudes.[34] Where moral judgments criss-cross and appear in agreement, this agreement takes place within the horizon of the different world-views. Nevertheless, through this criss-crossing, one comes upon cases of practical moral judgments that should be understood as having validity beyond the particular society in which they originate. These judgments derive their critical force from within their own tradition and from the degree to which multiple societies and communities criss-cross in their judgments.

X. Communities of discourse and institutionalized discourses

The emphasis on discourse and procedure underscores the importance of universalizing norms and judgments. Unfortunately, if discourse is treated much more formally and procedurally, then the institutional arrangements by which different persons and people enter into the discourse and principle within morality is neglected.[35] The problems that a deliberative democracy face within a specific nation also exist within a global situation, namely, problems of participation and equality within institutionalized forms of discourse. The uneducated, the poor, and minorities are often left outside the conversation, just as in a globalized world those negatively effected by the global economy have less of a say in the shaping of economic decisions. Although a discourse claims that its universalizable procedures would include these, it can only do so in so far that it incorporates within its very approach the thick understandings of themselves that culturally diverse and economically disadvantaged groups have.

Hence neither a world ethic nor a local ethic can deal with the globalized situation today. Instead one needs a conception of morality in relation to practical reasononing that seeks at the same time to bring into reflective equilibrium both the irreducible pluralism in religious and ethical world-views and the different interpretations of certain partially shared background experiences. This results not so much in a world ethic as a dialogue in which reflective judgment and diverse conceptions criss-cross in their moral reasoning and argumentation.

This article has argued that globalization entails paradoxical tendencies. That unification, universality and homogeneity go hand in hand with diversity, particularity and heterogeneity. In the face of globalization, there are currently particularist and universalist tendencies within ethical views stressing respectively either particularity and heterogeneity or universality and homogeneity. In contrast, I have argued for an understanding of morality as a practical rationality that takes the irudicibility of pluralism seriously at the same that it seeks to show how criss-crossing moral judgments begin to deal with the problems of globalization.

Notes

1. Guenther Roth, 'Global Capitalism and Multi-Ethnicity: Max Weber Then and Now' in *The Cambridge Companion to Weber*, Stephen Turner (ed), New York: Cambridge University Press 2000, pp.117–30.
2. Manuel Castells, *The Rise of the Network Society*, New York: Blackwell 1996.
3. For a survey of diverse theories of globalization, see Frederick Buell, *National Culture and the New Global System*, Baltimore, Md.: Johns Hopkins University Press 1994. See also Helmut Wiesenthal, 'Globalisierung, Soziologische und politikwissenschaftliche Koordination eines unbekannten Terrain', *Berliner Debatte – Initial* 7 (1966), pp.37ff.
4. Ulrich Beck, *What Is Globalization?*, New York: Blackwell 2000. Compare, however, Roland Robertson, *Globalization: Social Theory and Global Culture*, London 1992.
5. Francis Schüssler Fiorenza, 'Roman Catholic Fundamentalism: A Challenge to Theology' in *The Struggle over the Past: Fundamentalism in the Modern World*, William M. Shea. (ed), Lanham, M.D.: University Press of America 1991, pp. 231–54.
6. Homi K. Bhabha, 'On Cultural Choice' in *The Turn toward Ethics*, Marjorie Garber, Beatrice Hanssen and Rebecca L. Walkowitz (eds), New York: Routledge 2000, pp.181–200.
7. See Jean Baudrillard, *The Mirror of Production*, St Louis: Telos Press 1975 and *Selected Writings*, Mark Poster (ed), Stanford: Stanford University Press 1988.
8. Cf. Frederic Jameson and Masao Miyoshi (eds), *The Cultures of Globalization*, North Carolina: Duke University Press 2000 and, earlier, Frederic Jameson, *Signatures of the Visible*, London: Routledge 1990.
9. Richard Rorty, 'Global Utopias, History, and Philosophy' in *Cultural Pluralism, Identity and Globalization*' in Luiz Soares (ed), Rio de Janiero: UNESCO/ISSC/EDUCAM 1996, pp.457–69 reprinted as 'Globalization, the Politics of Identity and Social Hope' in Rorty's collection of essays, *Philosophy and Social Hope*, New York: Penguin 1996. See also Anindira Niyogi Balslev and Richard Rorty, *Cultural Otherness: Correspondence with Richard Rorty*, Atlanta: Scholars Press 1999.
10. The titles of two of his essays. The former is included in his *Philosophy and Social Hope*, p.80 and the latter in his *Objectivism, Relativism and Truth: Philosophical Papers*, Vol. 1, New York: Cambridge University Press 1989.
11. Ibid. See also Rorty's treatment of human rights in 'Human Rights, Rationality, and Sentimentality' in Richard Rorty, *Truth and Progress: Philosophical Papers*, Vol. 3, New York: Cambridge University Press 1998, pp.167–85.
12. *Philosphy and Social Hope*, p. 87.
13. For criticism of such a monolithic conception, see James Schmidt, 'What Enlightenment Project?', *Political Theory* 28 (2000), pp.734–57.
14. William Galston, 'Two Concepts of Liberalism', *Ethics* 105 (1995), pp.516–34.
15. A further issue that cannot be discussed here is Ronald Dworkin's suggestion

that liberalism is constituted through equality rather than freedom. Ronald M. Dworkin, *Taking Rights Seriously*, Cambridge, Mass.: Harvard University Press 1977.

16. Michael Walzer, *Spheres of Justice: A Defense of Pluralism and Equality*, New York: Basic Books 1983 and *Interpretation and Social Criticism*, Cambridge: Harvard University Press 1987. For a critical discussion of his work see David Miller (ed), *Pluralism, Justice, and Equality*, New York: Oxford University Press 1995.

17. Michael Walzer, *Thick and Thin: Moral Argument at Home and Abroad*, Notre Dame: University of Notre Dame Press 1994. For a critical, though sympathetic analysis of Walzer from the perspective of Jürgen Habmeras see Shane O'Neill, *Impartiality in Context: Grounding Justice in a Pluralist World*, Albany: SUNY 1997.

18. See Karl-Otto Apel, 'Globalization and the Need for Universal Ethics' in *European Journal of Social Theory* 3 (2000), pp.137–55. See also Karl-Otto Apel, *From a Transcendental-Semiotic Point of View*, New York: St Martin's Press 1998.

19. Habermas does not take over the centrality of Apel's appeal to an 'ultimate foundation'. For Habermas' theory in relation to global issues see Jürgen Habermas, *Between Facts and Norms: Contibutions to a Discourse Theory of Law and Democracy*, Cambridge: MIT Press 1996.

20. Ronald M. Dworkin, *A Matter of Principle*, Cambridge: Harvard University Press 1985; *Taking Rights Seriously*, Cambridge: Harvard University Press 1977; *Law's Empire*, Cambridge: Harvard University Press 1986; *Sovereign Virtue: The Theory and Practice of Equality*, Cambridge: Harvard University Press 2000.

21. Alan Gewirth, *The Community of Rights*, Chicago: University of Chicago Press 1996; *Human Rights: Essays on Justification and Applications*, Chicago: University of Chicago Press 1982; *Reason and Morality*, Chicago: University of Chicago Press 1978.

22. Compare John Rawls, *A Theory of Justice*, Cambridge: Harvard University Press 1971 with his later works, *Political Liberalism*, New York: Columbia University Press 1993; *Collected Papers*, Cambridge: Harvard University Press 1999; *The Law of Peoples*, Cambridge: Harvard University Press 1999; *Justice as Fairness*, Cambridge: Harvard University Press 2001.

23. See his criticism of the early Rawls in Otfried Höffe, *Gerichtigkeit als Fairness*, Freiburg/München 1977.

24. Reiner Wimmer, *Universalisierung in Der Ethik: Analyse, Kritik Und Rekonstruktion Ethischer Rationalitätsansprüche*, Frankfurt: Suhrkamp 1980.

25. See Hans Küng, *A Global Ethic for Global Politics and Economics*, New York and London 1997.

26. See Anthony J. Lisska's attempt to reconstruct and reconceive natural law theory in relation to the work Henry B. Veatch and John Finnis in his *Aquinas's*

Theory of Natural Law: An Analytic Reconstruction, Oxford: Clarendon Press 1996.

27. For general survey of ethical positions in the debate between more particular and more universal approaches see Rainer Forst, *Kontexte Der Gerechtigkeit: Politische Philosophie Jenseits von Liberalismus und Kommunitarismus*, Frankfurt: Suhrkamp 1994; Walter Reese-Schäfer, *Grengötter Der Moral. Der Neuere Europäisch-Amerikanische Diskurs Zur Politischen Ethik*, Frankfurt: Suhrkamp 1997; Yong Huang, *Religious Goodness and Political Rightness: Beyond the Liberal Communitarian Debate*, Francis Schüssler Fiorenza and Peter Machinist (eds), Harvard Theological Studies 49, Harrisburg, Pa: Trinity Press International 2001.

28. Dietmar Mieth, *Moral Und Erfahrung : Beiträge Zur Theologisch-Ethischen Hermeneutik*, Freiburg, Herder 1977.

29. Onora O'Neill's essay 'Four Models of Practical Reasoning' in her *Bounds of Justice*, New York: Cambridge University Press 2000. See also her attempt to overcome the conflict between universalism and particularism in moral theories, *Towards Justice and Virtue: A Constructive Account of Practical Reasoning*, New York: Cambridge University Press 1996.

30. See Francis Schüssler Fiorenza, 'Justice and Charity in Social Welfare' in *Who Will Provide? The Changing Role of Religion in American Social Welfare*, Mary Jo Bane, Brent Coffin and Ronald Thiemann (eds), Boulder: Westview 2000, pp. 73–96.

31. See John Gray, *Isaiah Berlin*, Princeton: Princeton University Press 1996, pp.38–75. See also the review and corrections by Michael Walzer in *New York Review of Books* (2001).

32. Martha Craven Nussbaum, *Sex & Social Justice*, New York: Oxford University Press 1999 and *Women and Human Development: The Capabilities Approach*, New York: Cambridge University Press 2000.

33. See Arthur Kleinman, *Writing at the Margin: Discourse Between Anthropology and Medicine*, Berkeley: University of California Press 1995.

34. I have deliberately selected 'criss-crossing judgment' rather than the term 'overlapping consensus', for the latter term as used by Rawls refers to common beliefs and shared standards within civic society that provide stability for the political institutions. It does not sufficently address the difference and variety of hierarchy of values.

35. Francis Schüssler Fiorenza, 'Politische Theologie Und Liberale Gerechtigkeits-Konzeption' in *Mystik Und Politik. Johann Baptist Metz Zu Ehren*, Edward Schillebeeckx (ed), Mainz: Matthias Grünewald 1988, pp.105–17.

III. Applications

Global Business and the Global Ethic

HANS KÜNG

I. Global ethic: not a consequence of globalization

In October 2000, at a colloquium with Chinese scholars in Peking on 'Global Ethic and Chinese Tradition', I was asked whether talk of a global ethic was not a necessary consequence of globalization. In China the term 'globalization' (like the term 'capitalism' previously), has predominantly negative connotations and is identified with Americanization and Western domination which destroy a people's own culture and tradition. However, I was able gently to point out that I had already been using the term 'global ethic' for many years and that the Global Ethic Project had developed (in 1990 with my book *Global Responsibility*)[1] before the term 'globalization' was used at all.

Of course, the globalization of the economy, technology and communication has given talk of a global ethic a new urgency. For more than ever this globalization has generated new forms of a globalization of problems and thus formally calls for a globalization of ethics. To this degree, while the global ethic is not grounded in globalization, globalization becomes an extremely urgent task. This is true not least for those active in the sphere of the global economy and global finance.

I would want to maintain the four characteristics of globalization which I presented in *A Global Ethic for Global Politics and Economics* (1997), since they can be the basis for a rational consensus between those who affirm globalization and those who oppose it. Globalization is:

1. unavoidable, unstoppable, irreversible: it is made possible by the abolition of the division of the world into East and West and above all by technological innovations like the global flow of data, the World Wide Web and electronic global stock exchanges;

2. ambivalent: with winners and losers, with individuals, businesses, locations, nations and regions which rise and fall;

3. unpredictable: with intended main effects and unintentional side effects, with economic miracles and debacles, long-term business forecasts (leaving aside the political order) which are hardly more accurate than the long-term weather forecasts;

4. controllable: globalization is not a natural phenomenon like an earthquake or a weather front but can be influenced and controlled – though only within limits – by national governments, central banks and international institutions. In fact in recent years a whole series of measures of a political order have been implemented or at least considered by the IMF and the World Bank, by the G7 finance ministers and by the Financial Stability Forum.

From this I would like to derive the thesis that the global market calls for a solid global framework within the political order, a global market framework which the market itself cannot provide and which in turn calls for a global ethic. There is a need to reflect on this afresh in the face of a 'new economy' which has recently appeared. I offer these reflections not as a professional economist but as an involved observer of our time, driven by concern for the future of the global economy. Some deliberately exaggerated formulations, provocative sketches and direct demands arise out of an ethically-based responsibility for the common good of whole regions and nations, but also of business itself.

II. 'New Economics'? New 'economy' but no new 'economics'

The late 1990s have again intensified the urgent need for a global ethic. This has happened through what is often mistakenly called the 'new economics', though some economists doubtingly ask whether there has ever been such a thing, because it has grown old so quickly. We must make distinctions.

Beyond question there are new information and communication technologies which have brought epoch-making upheavals to the global economy as far as China and India. The key terms here are the Internet economy, e-commerce, the information society, world-wide networking and the free flow of global information. All this has resulted in fundamental changes in forms of organization and business practice and to this degree in a new economy.

But do these new information and communication technologies bring with them a new set of economic laws? Do they simply rob the old economic principles of their force? Do they lead to new business theory, a new science of business, and in this sense a new economics? Not at all. Nevertheless some Wall Street experts proclaimed a new 'economic model' all over the world: business growth without inflation and an endless boom on the stock exchange. It was thought old-fashioned to suppose that there were physical limits to growth. At the beginning of the year 2000, the *Wall Street Journal* stated that in a knowledge-based economy there were no constraints. The old rule that one should buy shares at favourable prices so as to become rich when the profits of the business rose would thus no longer apply. One could buy confidently and with no fear; the boom and bust cycle had been abolished in principle; in principle share values would constantly rise.

However, these dreams have been shattered in the first two years of the new millennium and so it has become evident that while the new technology, along with changed forms of organization and business practices, has created a new economy as such, in principle there are no new economics, no new business theory or business science. Boom and bust has not been abolished. As in previous decades, even large increases in production cannot prevent a recession. For not only inflation but also excessive private consumption and speculative business investments can lead to a recession.

III. Bubble-economy: a virtual reality, not a real one

So in the end those warning voices proved right which kept on asserting that the boom sparked off by the 'new economics' was a 'bubble economy' driven on by speculation. In fact the 'new economics' proved to be a purely 'virtual' reality, an optimistic and fanciful projection, as it were confined to the screens of the stock exchange, which was based on a mood in the international financial world far removed from 'real' reality. The magic of technology and a free market in many ways proved to be sheer 'magic' – with Internet firms which had been founded not as businesses to provide services but as so to speak virtual joint-stock companies.

The real consequences have been serious: in the USA the consumer boom of past years has led to a decline in the personal rate of savings to virtually nil and to an investment boom by businesses – both with the expectation that things will keep going on like this. But in the year 2000 more than 140 dot.com firms suddenly went bankrupt, often firms with no real resources, no profits and often even with no products, firms only with fantastic prophecies for the future. In the face of the falling stock exchange, high levels of debt and anxieties about jobs, private consumption too is experiencing a collapse: many consumers are losing confidence and often also their nerves.

Happy indebtedness threatens to turn into anxious saving, which can stall the boom, as is especially evident in Japan.

IV. Research into causes: rational and irrational motivations

What are the deeper reasons for this stock market fever? Particularly if one is in favour of a free (and social) market economy, one may not overlook the fact that it is those involved, those who are supposed always to act 'rationally', who are responsible for the dot.com disaster. Reality looks different from what it is in economic mainstream theory. There are:

• entrepreneurs, who founded firms without the necessary basis and made euphoric forecasts;
• venture capitalists, who financed them without requiring the usual guarantees;
• investment bankers, who launched businesses on the stock exchange which often were not ready for it;
• financial analysts and the media, who gave uncritical approval and fired up the stock market fever.

What was the motivation behind all this drive? It is not enough to point out the arrogance and ignorance of the smart online entrepreneurs, who were usually young and had little experience of the world, and who impatiently attempted to move everything along more rapidly than is normally possible for people with their fixed habits; who knew about the highly complex mechanisms of the new technologies but not about those of commerce and so were incapable of having the right goods at the right place at the right time. Such an analysis of motivation does not go far enough.

Here we must address not only rational but also completely irrational motivations. Contrary to the basic assumption of mainstream economists that in business people always act out of rational, unemotional self-interest, a more recent trend in American research among behavioural economists, which also incorporates psychology, makes it clear that in business, too, people time and again act irrationally, even on the basis of emotional hunches and false arguments, out of self-gratification and arrogance, sometimes in a quite incomprehensible and destructive way. Business, too, is evidently not a purely rational, self-regulating system, which like physical reality can be explained, calculated and controlled by mathematical equations. For example, these behavioural economists explain the typically American overspending and undersaving by the fact that most people, despite all previous rational considerations and the best intentions, like to spend money as soon as they really have it in their hands – not very differently from in a casino.

Thus the stock exchange often corresponds less to economic reality than to the mood of the investors: their behaviour as a herd, the over-estimation of their capacity for forecasts, their antipathy to selling falling shares and thus making a loss. George Soros is right: the markets are driven by greed and fear, by greed for yet more, and fear of losing it again. With some justice it has been called casino capitalism.

This particular insight allows us to research really deeply into causes: what do the smart businessmen and women of the new economics have in common with the equally smart venture capitalists, investment bankers and financial analysts? What is the catalyst for this whole stock market fever? It is not just the pursuit of gain, which in principle is justified, but the greed for profit, for quick money, easy money. New issues were understood as a licence to print money. New economic models and strategies were immediately developed from this greed for money: as if the stockmarket always went upwards, as if the boom and bust cycle had been abolished, as if there were never-ending gains and never serious crashes.

This irrational greed for short-term gains ('shareholder value') and quick money was rationally justified by some ultraliberal theories which no longer had in view the freedom of the individual over against absolutist rulers or a state with excessive regulations, as at the beginning of liberalism, but the purely economic self-interest of the individual in the free market, which could celebrate its triumph in the age of Reagan and Thatcher, as if it would automatically bring in universal prosperity without state intervention. Here von Mises and von Hayek already pointed to greed, carelessness and exaggeration. Is the ethic of business thus reduced to the 'moral obligation' to increase profit? 'The business of business is business.' Is there no social responsibility for the common good? In the USA today the communitarian movement opposes this. In fact the involvement of countless people in the environmental movement, voluntary activities and many other enterprises for the common good can only be explained by an 'supra-rational' action which is not simply bound up with self-interest but is governed by altruism, loyalty, fairness, benevolence and gratitude – 'non-hedonistic action'. But at the same time there is the other side, governed by egotism. And this makes me raise a critical question which goes beyond questions of business and financial policy.

V. The stock exchange and morality: are lying and deceit allowed?

The 'shareholder-value approach' and the greed for quick money has in recent years driven many people in the business world to set themselves above elementary commandments of humanity. We need only note some facts. There has been lying, fraud, theft and false witness on a grand scale from people from which one would not have expected it. For:

- It is lying when the directors of a firm (e.g. EM-TV, Gigabell) give information about the state of their business to shareholders which is too late, all too rosy or even false.
- It is also lying where the profits are manipulated to achieve a higher share price, where concealed payments in the form of (outstanding) stock options do not appear in any profit and loss account, or even specific costs are simply left out of a firm's accounts (in the case of Amazon the net loss in 2000 was four times as great as indicated, namely $1.4 billion).
- There is false witness when businesses buy back their own shares at gigantic prices so as artificially to drive the share price higher, in fact at the expense of the family silver: measures which lead to a squeezing of the balance sheets, so that in a crisis there are no silent reserves as a bolster, and a crash becomes almost unavoidable.
- People are misled when, as in the USA, the statistical calculation of the Gross National Product is made on the 'hedonistic' price index, which includes increases in productivity, and a picture of actual economic growth is given which is clearly exaggerated in a positive direction. The same is true where businesses with high rates of growth attempt to conceal the lower profits which should now govern the share price.
- It is theft when financial analysts on Wall Street and elsewhere simply become underhand self-interested sellers of shares who with pseudo-research recommended the buying of shares (especially those of their own investment house) and thus piled up millions even when the share prices were already in free fall and their customers were losing billions. For example, at the end of 2000 the 'Queen of the Internet', Mary Meeker, who earned $15 million for the e-com companies in 1999 with her fore-casts, was still giving all 11 Internet shares (8 of them launched by her own investment bank Morgan Stanley) the buy recommendation 'outperform', although overall they had fallen by an average 83%. In Germany, too, analysts are thought to intensify trends rather than set them.

In addition to the financial political problems of globalization, there are the social problems, which also occur at a world level. Precisely because I saw the positive results of globalization threatened, some years ago I already felt that I should issue a warning:

> Should the supreme criterion in the present process of globalization prove to be the maximization of profit, and should that alone prevail, we must be prepared for serious social conflicts and crises. The present strength of capital and the weakness of the trade unions should not mislead us here. For we cannot assume that society as a whole would accept a lapse into nineteenth-century liberalism and pure capitalism without putting up any resistance.[2]

At the same time I referred to the United States, where after the boom of the 1920s, the 1929 crash and the subsequent Great Depression under President Franklin D. Roosevelt, the American welfare state was built up by the New Deal in opposition to *laissez faire*.

The protests of the opponents of globalization in Seattle, Washington, Prague, Davos and Anti-Davos (Porto Alegre in Brazil), which include students, trade unionists, Greens and church people, are to be taken seriously, and they have confirmed this warning. Of course attempts should be made to prevent violent outbursts from anarchists, but in Davos excessive police regulations so strongly limited freedom of travel, the right to demonstrate and freedom of opinion, contrary to all Swiss tradition, that even many Swiss were made all the more aware of the problems. The international institutions (WTO, IMF and the World Bank) should also react positively to the globalized protests and ensure that there is more transparency in their decision-making processes and thus more responsibility in their organizations; in some circumstances NGOs could also be admitted as observers.

It is welcome that the founder president of the World Economic Forum, Professor Klaus Schwab, thinks that over the next year efforts should be made towards a more intensive dialogue with the NGOs and that here again the values of the European 'social market economy' should be brought more into play. His view is that so far businesses have not given a convincing answer to the erosion of the concepts of security and predictability in human life, or to the problems which are created by the elevation of success and competition to the status of values.

On the other hand, in the financial crisis in South-East Asia those who control large sums of money, the managers of pension funds and investment funds, had the experience that it is not enough to aim at high short-term yields. In the middle and long term it is also important for partners to keep to their contracts and be reliable; for a society to be minimally prone to corruption; for the banks to be solid and for the political institutions to function. All these are political and ethical questions which show that performance really is not everything: a responsibility for the common good with an ethical foundation is necessary both for business and the state.

Finally, the trade unions in no way simply oppose globalization, but adopt a differentiated standpoint. Bill Jordan, General Secretary of the Confederation of Free Trade Unions, has put it like this:

> The international labour movement is not against globalization; indeed we would agree that globalization can be a big part of the answer to the problem of the world's poor. But it is also a big part of the problem . . . The labour movement's position is simply that the rules governing globalization should protect the interests of the poor and not just the rich, and that the benefits of increased trade and increased global output should be shared by all.[3]

This basic standpoint is doubtless shared by many. Not only social democratic governments but also 'compassionate conservatives' like Aznar or Schüssel might subscribe to the formula of a 'progressive equation' with which the heads of government Tony Blair, Wim Kok, Göran Persson and Gerhard Schröder have defined their position in the discussion on globalization: 'globalization + welfare'. However, this needs to be made more concrete and precise.

VI. The global market requires a global framework

We turn first to the problems of the globalized financial market. If today more currency circulates round the globe than in the whole of world trade over four months, in my view one should not declare that the world-wide capital markets are a catalyst for transparency, business efficiency and democratic control. Where is the transparency, the economic efficiency and the democratic control here?

Didn't this 'global market' without any frontiers, constraints and regulations itself make possible the Asian crisis, with effects which have by no means yet been overcome? Doesn't this completely unregulated market with its short-term speculative investments undermine the long-term industrial investments, which usually produce a lower yield? Doesn't the new preference for big customers by the big banks undermine the financial liquidity of medium and small businesses and in time disturb the social peace on which the big banks also depend? Doesn't this development also undermine the trust in the system of the market economy that we need? Indeed, doesn't it put the very stability of the world financial system in question?

After the latest currency crises in Mexico, South-East Asia, Russia, South America and Turkey, even mainstream economists concede that there are serious weaknesses in the international currency system (defective bank supervision, transparency and surveillance, a meshing of the state and private sectors, and nepotism). Is there to be further 'bail out' by the IMF as in Mexico, continued 'carry trade' as in Japan? There is certainly a need for commerce: we need a new order in the global financial system. It is hard to see why air traffic, which has become immensely complex and dangerous, needs some elementary rules and controls which are accepted world-wide, and the international traffic in money, which is just as complex and dangerous in its own way, does not.

Is it sufficient here to speak only of a 'reinforcement of the international financial system'? Isn't it time to create a new 'global financial architecture', an expression also used by President Clinton and his finance minister Robert Rubin at the height of the South-East Asian financial crisis, which of course does not mean that everything was wrong in the previous international financial architecture? At that time Klaus Schwab also made a demand:

> We need more global rules, first of all for investments which cross frontiers. Moreover we need a world environment authority. The International Monetary Fund should develop the financial architecture world-wide. The International Labour Organization should create world-wide mechanisms for working standards. The problem lies less with the businesses than with the states. They have to give up some of their sovereignty.[4]

Many mainstream economists reject reform measures which go further, like a global insurance agency for debts (George Soros), a world central bank (Jeffrey Sacs), an international super-regulator (Henry Kaufman), a single world currency (Richard Cooper) or a minimal tax on currency exchange (James Tobin and Lawrence Summers). There are well-founded objections to all these reform measures. But particularly if one warns that there is insufficient political substructure for such measures, one cannot stop there.

Thus when after horrific losses (estimated at $350 billion in the case of the crisis in Asia and Russia) the big banks confess themselves content with repair measures like better information, transparency, communication and supervision, one asks whether individual measures are adequate here. In view of the chronic currency crises, mainstream economists too concede that the financial architecture is the weakest link in the chain and to this degree is itself a cause of crisis. So here, is not something like a new, indeed a novel, Bretton Woods agreement needed, which not least clearly defines the Bretton Woods institutions, the IMF (a monetary institution) and the World Bank (a development organization), and at the same time gives them supplementary functions? Unfortunately, so far we have found no towering economic architects of the stature of John Maynard Keynes, who at that time worked out the theoretical framework for the coherent resolutions at Bretton Woods. Certainly, though, there are expert reports on rebuilding the architecture of international finance. The finance ministers of G7 looked at them only briefly in Palermo. Will perhaps effective decisions in the right direction be made in July in Genoa at the G8 (G7 + Russia) summit?

Here attention needs to be paid to the problems of poverty in developing and threshold countries, which recently have also come to be taken seriously in the economy – as the *Washington Post* wrote:

Recovery in the share, bond and currency markets does not mean the same thing as recovery for the ordinary people who have suffered most from the collapses of the last 21 months. Many members of the middle class have been thrown into poverty and many poor families have become even poorer. Their recovery will take years yet. Their suffering and shattered hopes must remain a central concern for the financial politicians of the developed countries.[5]

This raises ethical questions which are now also being taken very seriously by the World Bank (combating poverty) and the IMF (monetary stability).

In addition to currency policy, trade policy also plays a decisive role in a global framework. After more than fifty years the international community has finally managed to make an institution, WTO, out of a treaty, GATT. There is liberalization not only for commodities but also for services and the protection of intellectual property. An improved process for settling disputes, the incorporation of multiphase agreements, and so on, are steps in liberalization which document the moral obligation of the industrial countries towards the developing countries. But already many countries – industrial countries, but also developing countries – are again evading regulations they themselves have made. The average duty on industrial products is around 3%. But the 'new protectionism' which focusses protectionist measures on a country or on a product, contrary to the word and spirit of the WTO, keeps putting out new shoots. Similarly, over recent years countries have increasingly banded together in free trade areas; these may be allowed in the WRO, but they go against the multilateral abolition of trade restrictions proper.

Ethical perspectives play no role in a 'strategic trade policy' in which each is his own neighbour. Section 301 of the US trade law, which is used by the USA as a potential threat, is one of the best examples of this. The conference of ministers in Seattle in December 1999 did not fail simply because of the protesters outside. If not even the industrial countries can agree on the way in which they carry on trade, and if already in the forefront there are open conflicts not only between industrial and developing countries but also among the developing countries themselves, what hope is there for globalization in the sense of a liberalization which in the long term will benefit every state? Only if international trade is liberalized as far as possible and the goals set by WTO are moved will it be possible for ethical aspects to play a role.

VII. A global framework for the market requires a global ethic

In a personal conversation in New Delhi in autumn 1997 about whether an exchange rate tax could be implemented, Robert McNamara, for many years president of the World Bank, told me that it could, 'If you want it.' In fact, if a global or reinforced financial architecture – which for example also included the private sector, or more precisely the home institutions of the banks active internationally in the resolution of crises – were to be aimed at (on the basis of an initiative from the USA, the EU and Japan), then it would need the political will of those responsible. And in enterprises for the common good of the people which cost sweat and require sacrifices, and in some circumstances also a sacrifice of state sovereignty, this is hardly possible without an ethical impulse, without the moral drive, the moral energy which was shown over the Marshall Plan, the drafting of a Universal Declaration of Human Rights or the founding of a united Europe.

I have emphasized some negative aspects of the developments without disputing the positive ones; different views are quite possible about the details of this analysis, and in any case the situation is extremely difficult to interpret. However, my concern is the conclusion that anyone who wants the global market must also want a framework in the political order, a global framework for the market. That does not mean interventionism which sets out to do away with the mechanisms of the market, nor does it mean just a bundle of corrective individual measures which can only serve as a palliative, but rather a coherent set of regulations and measures in the political order (cf. Bretton Woods) which are opposed to a liberalization of the movement of capital at any price and yet do not represent a lapse into foreign exchange control.

Here we are not concerned just with specifically economic questions. These are highly political and ultimately also ethical questions, questions which concern the whole of society. Specifically the question is, say, whether the pursuit of profit, which is in principle justified, should be the one and only purpose of the economy, a bank, a business. The phenomenon of economic globalization makes it clear that there must also be a globalization in ethics. Anyone who wants this global framework for the market must also want, indeed presuppose, a global ethic. 'Global markets need global frameworks based upon global ethics in order to orient a globalized economy towards sustainable development for the benefit of all' (this is also the aim of the various organizations in the 'Global Society Dialogue' initiated by Professor F. J. Rademacher of Ulm).

We were given important support for this vision by the new Director General of the IMF, Horst Köhler, at the annual meeting in Prague in 2000. There he recalled the appeal by President Václav Havel 'to reflect on the wider dimension of the task, to allow globalization to work for the prosperity of all, to seek new sources of a sense of responsibility for the world'. And Dr Köhler added: 'I fully share this call for generally recognized moral standards. Indeed, as Hans Küng says, a global economy needs a global ethic.'

Of course the global ethic does involve financial markets and the politics of commerce but also technological, social, cultural and ecological problem areas and frameworks. It also involves developments like the deciphering of human heredity (the genome project). This offers hopes of therapy for hereditary illnesses – a great opportunity also for businesses and their share-holders. But it also leads to fear of dangerous interventions in heredity which could finally be at the expense of human dignity, indeed of the prosperity of humankind. There is a growing need for regulation not only in gene research but also in other areas: this is a challenge to politics, but also presupposes good will and a responsible attitude in all involved.

The world-wide crisis in moral orientation which is developing with the headlong process of modernization and the retreat of religious ties makes it clear that a reflection on the necessary minimum of specific ethical values, basic attitudes and criteria is urgently needed, a global ethic for this global society and global economy, to which all nations and all interest groups could and should commit themselves. A framework for the financial markets must have global validity. But a basic ethical consensus must also have global validity, so that a somewhat more humane, peaceful and just society on our globe is guaranteed. I want to clarify this.

VIII. The presupposition of the market economy is an intact civil society

Globalization, particularly if one is in favour of it, is far more than just an economic concept. In order to make the globalization of markets, technology and communication sustainable, the gains in the economy associated with it must be focussed in a way which is compatible with society and the environment; social and environmental standards must be taken into account. Here reflection on global ethical standards is absolutely necessary.

Today's globalization differs from earlier forms of development of the global economy which were brought about by free-trade agreements: the rapidly expanding progress in the technologies has set in motion a completely novel dynamic. This has brought about changes for all national economies and many of their spheres in the problems which have to be dealt with, in the number of partners involved and in some rules of the game. All parties which are active internationally are affected by these changes and have to react to them. To guarantee that the economic achievement remains subordinate to humane and social goals, globalization needs a political basis and an ethical framework.

There are certainly no easy and quick solutions for the complicated problems connected with globalization. The process which leads to global solutions includes communication between all concerned on the same level, acceptance of the perspective of other peoples, and the quest for a consensus which is in the interest of all parties, supported by an ethic of responsibility. However, recent experiences throughout the world and not least in Russia have shown that the market economy develops its desired effect only if it is based on an intact democratic civil society which rests on basic values and fundamental ethical standards embracing both rights and responsibilities. Once again, the four heads of government mentioned above remarked:

> We need to strengthen civil society. Civil society is a check against overweening government and untrammelled market power. The underlying values should be clear – a society open and inclusive, but based on responsibilities as well as rights.[6]

However, in view of the globalization and deregulation of the markets and the principle of economic competition which is increasingly also dominating international relations, over and above any national features, explicit attention must also be paid to the global dimensions of a social and ecological market economy which still has to be created. So in the ninth section I return to the basic statement of the first section: the global market requires a global ethic.

IX. The Global Ethic Project

One often hears questions like: Are values still valid in the age of postmodern randomness – and if so, what are they? Who is to set 'global rules for the game'? Whose values and norms are these? First of all my answer is in general terms and states a principle:

- These global values and rules do not need to be set but have already been set.
- These values and norms can be found in the great religious and philosophical traditions of humankind which have been handed down over millennia.

In other words, today we do not need to re-invent the wheel of ethics, but need only to use it properly. For if so many institutions and forums are now developing standards – and, as I mentioned at the beginning, there are more than fifty codes of conduct in the sphere of financial market stability alone – then, as Jürgen Stark points out, 'initially no "more" stability has yet been achieved. The decisive thing is to apply these standards and make sure that they are also observed.' The implementation in fact presupposes some very elementary values, standards and attitudes, traces of which can be followed back to the humanization of men and women. They make up the basic substratum of a shared ethic of humankind which also applies today, as formulated in the Global Ethic Project.

When my book *Global Responsibility. In Search of a New World Ethic* was published (in German in 1990, in English in 1991), I could refer to hardly any documents by global organizations on a global ethic. Granted, there were declarations of human rights, above all that made by the United Nations in 1948, but there were no declarations on human responsibilities. However, just three years after the appearance of *Global Responsibility* came the proclamation of the Global Ethic Declaration of the Parliament of the World's Religions (1993). And now, ten years later, there are already several important international documents which not only acknowledge human rights but explicitly speak of human responsibilities, indeed which programmatically call for a global ethic and even already attempt to make it specific:

1. The great 1995 report by the UN Commission for Global Governance calls for 'an ethic of neighbourliness' in all areas: 'global values must be the core of a world political order'.
2. The equally important report by the World Commission on Culture and Development, also from 1995, also calls in the very first chapter for 'a New Global Ethic', an ethic of humankind, a global ethic 'to cope with the global problems mentioned'.
3. This request also found support in the UNESCO Universal Ethics Project of 1997, the World Economic Forum at Davos in 1997 and the Indira Gandhi Conference in Delhi in 1997.

Such international conferences and commissions not only stress the need for a global ethic but also in part call for a formulation of human responsibilities. This was first done in 1993 by the Parliament of the World's Religions in the Global Ethic Declaration already mentioned, and by the InterAction Council, made up of former heads of state and prime ministers, which on 1 September 1997 published a proposal for a Universal Declaration of Human Responsibilities.[7]

Both declarations are based on two fundamental demands of humanity, the specific application of which changes the atmosphere in every institute, office, factory and business. First, 'Every person, of no matter what sex, ethnic origin, language, age, nationality or religion has a responsibility to treat all human beings humanely.' And secondly there is the Golden Rule of all the great religious and ethical traditions, which also has to apply between nations: 'What you do not want done to yourself, do not do to others.'

Four irrevocable directives build on this; they can be found in all the religious and ethical traditions of humankind and particularly in a situation of change to modernity need to be translated. This is done in the documents.

- The responsibility for a culture of non-violence and respect for all life: have respect for life. Again the age-old instruction, do not kill!
- The responsibility for a culture of solidarity and a just economic order: deal justly and fairly. Again the age-old instruction, do not steal!
- The responsibility for a culture of toleration and a life in truthfulness: speak and act truthfully. Again the age-old instruction, do not lie!

- The responsibility for a culture of equal rights and the partnership of men and women: respect and love one another. Again the age-old instruction, do not abuse sexuality!

These elementary ethical norms are focussed on voluntary commitment in the economic sphere as well. Here, however, there is not just an individual but at the same time a social ethic. It is certainly true that since the beginning of modernity, moral forces have been at work in the natural sciences, technology, business and democracy and later too have watched over their humanitarian orientation and efficiency. There is therefore rightly talk of a morality which so to speak has entered our institutions and systems, a 'systematic morality' which affects all those involved in the present system (science, technology, business, politics).

But what would be the morality of the system without the morality of its subjects? What would be the morality of the institutions without the morality of the persons? In recent years there has been evidence enough of what can happen to our institutions if an important functionary has no conscience. There is no question about it: the functionality of institutions depends on the integrity of persons.

X. Ethical competence

Only those who themselves have an ethic can set down clear guidelines for others, as strong leadership requires: through values obligatory on all, by presenting goals, by the consistent observance of standards and the adoption of a quite definite attitude. Or, as I once heard the trustee of another foundation, the highly successful head of a global business, Prof. Reinhold Würth, say: whether a business is run more in the style of a big family or a strictly rational organization or a monarchical hierarchy, the decisive presupposition for its survival and its long-term success is 'integrity'. To be specific, this means that one can rely on the firm in every respect, that one is never bamboozled, deceived, has the wool pulled over one's eyes, but with due competence is always treated respectfully and honestly. In my introduction I already explained how immoral leadership of businesses does not pay in the long term.

Business leaders should see that there is conscious reflection on the question of ethics, which is often present among their management only in a latent and diffuse way. This should be done in the awareness that among today's business leaders, too, the kind of spirit that prevails in a business still depends heavily on individuals and above all on the managing director and the board. So here is a sketch of what goes to make up the ethical competence of the head of a business, presupposing economic and business competence.

Anyone who has to steer a big and sometimes unwieldy ship in bad visibility through a stormy sea – and time and again there are navigational errors, at great cost to human life and environmental damage – now has navigational instruments on board to make all the measurements and calculations necessary to plan the voyage in the very best way and to see that the ship reaches its destination as quickly as possible, with the minimum fuel and the maximum security. Today's 'integrated' navigation even uses more measuring instruments than are absolutely necessary to achieve maximum accuracy and safety and to bring all information immediately to the bridge.

But even the navigator, captain, steersman or pilot with the most modern equipment is always dependent on a chart. This contains unalterable coordinates, is drawn to a scale, and marks the directions north and south as these are irrevocably given by the compass. Only on this basis can the immediate position and the course to be taken be clearly defined and the necessary decisions be rightly made.

The metaphor does not need much explanation. Anyone who today has to guide a global business (in the face of a considerably more uncertain future than has been analysed in my account) through the storms of globalization and who has not only partial but possibly total responsibility for the course of the business, has in particular to guard against navigational errors, given the complexity of the details. Such a person similarly has on the bridge a wealth of technical, financial and organizational information and aids for constantly setting the right position and taking the right course. Indeed the project is often presented on a screen with different options – supported by statistics, graphics and forecasts – for a decision to be made. And for such a decision beyond doubt an analytical capacity, decisiveness and an executive ability are required; complex connections have to be identified in the shortest possible time and the right colleagues and resources brought to bear.

But in running a business, too, in addition to technical and organization equipment and a solid psychological constitution, other things are needed – to take up my metaphor again.

1. A clear awareness of the destination: what I mean is the final goal of the business, which is not just the necessary profit for the business and the prosperity of the shareholders, but the well-to-do of all stakeholders, agents and staff , including the customers, staff and suppliers, all who have a stake in the business and its environs. Indeed the entrepreneurial

goal should be seen against the horizon of the whole of society, which embraces the well-being of the national economy, state and society. Here a global business is expected to contribute to the advancement of the common good in a number of ways (for example by providing jobs, paying taxes and sponsoring culture);

2. A chart: what I mean is orientation that is more than pure knowledge, that in a holistic perspective maintains an overall view and makes it possible to set a realistic course.

3. A system of co-ordinates: what I mean are unalterable ethical standards which apply globally: what one may not ever do or must always do, whether in Germany or the USA, in Japan, India or Africa. The criterion of the standards is the principle of humanity stated above, combined with the Golden Rule.

4. A compass: what I mean is a conscience which functions incorruptibly, even in upheavals and changes of direction (mergers, take-overs, slimming down, relocations, mismanagement), which is the decisive factor in important decisions in the harsh reality of everyday business.

Awareness of the destination, orientation, ethical standards and an inner compass, these are all the structural elements of the ethic: not ethics as a doctrine, but the ethic as an inner moral attitude.

XI. How is a global ethic to be established?

This is a question which I am asked time and again, and certainly not only by sceptics. My answer is: in precisely the same way as the demands of the UN Global Compacts, which have now attained UNO status at least as demands. But what a long process of conscientization it has taken for human rights, humane working conditions and environmental demands to reach the level of UNO! In all these questions, as in the cases of peace and disarmament and the partnership between man and woman, a very complex and long process of a change of awareness has been needed. As such, this is already a presupposition for a change of human awareness in the direction of an ethic for humankind.

Many people can help here: pioneer thinkers, activists and initiative groups, but equally the countless teachers, from kindergarten to secondary school, who are now already committed to a new understanding of the world religions, global peace and a global ethic. Reflection on the ethic that all men and women have in common is more than ever necessary for the peaceful co-existence of humankind, at a local level (in countless multi-cultural and multi-faith cities) and at a global level (in terms of global communication, global economy, global ecology and global politics).[8]

So what happens in an individual's sphere of life, larger or smaller, depends on that individual and his or her motivation. When I asked the generous founder of our Global Ethic Foundation, Count von der Groeben, what motivated his commitment, he took our his wallet and showed me a little yellowed piece of paper containing a saying of Mahatma Gandhi about the 'seven social sins in today's world'. These are:

• Wealth without work,
• enjoyment without conscience,
• knowledge without character,
• business without morality,
• science without humanity,
• religion without sacrifice, and
• politics without principles.

Translated by John Bowden

Notes

1. Hans Küng, *Global Responsibility*, London and New York 1991.
2. Hans Küng, *A Global Ethic for Global Politics and Economics*, London and New York 1997, p.168.
3. *International Herald Tribune*, 21 December 2000.
4. *Die Zeit*, 27 January 2000.
5. *Washington Post*, 26 April 1999.
6. *International Herald Tribune*, 7 September 2000.
7. Hans Küng and Helmut Schmidt (eds), *A Global Ethic and Global Responsibilities. Two Declarations*, London 1998.
8. See here also Hans Küng and Karl-Josef Kuschel (eds), *Wissenschaft und Weltethos*, Munich 1998.

'Globalization' from the Perspective of Business Ethics*

FRIEDHELM HENGSBACH

I. Introduction

What can be the use of an ethical reflection which goes beyond sociological analyses of the phenomenon that is termed globalization? Can it add a methodologically original pattern of interpretation to these analyses? Four objections are often made to ethical reflection on globalization:

1. Modern societies, which are differentiated into partial systems, assign to ethical reflection the task of 'warning against morality'.[1] For such societies are not held together by a universally acknowledged morality. Law or commerce are governed by functional codes which are morally indifferent. A communication with moral connotations would merely alarm the partial systems and not integrate them into society.
2. Moreover ethical reflection seems to get torn apart in the contrast between an argument in terms of conviction ethics and an argument in terms of the ethics of responsibility, since while critical questions to businesses may seem well meant, they can prove counter-productive because of their unforeseeable and unintentional effects.[2]
3. However, if ethical reflection incorporates such consequences for action, it makes itself superfluous, for the economic principle of the cost-benefit comparison of the alternative use of scarce material is a 'fact of reason' and applies to any decision. What is economically reasonable accords with what is enjoined morally if as many consequences and side-effects as possible are taken into account.[3]
4. The structures and processes of globalization ask too much of an ethic which seeks to show how the action of subjects can be guided along the path of virtue.

Ethical reflection which attempts to avoid such objections[4] must first be sure of its location in practice: from what perspectives are the processes and structures of globalization being considered? Then it must take care to co-ordinate sociological analysis and reflection on social ethics: what sociological paradigms prove convincing from the perspective of the agents involved? How are hypotheses about society from system theory to be related to hypotheses from decision theory? And finally, those in particular social milieux, who are at the same time members of pluralist societies, will be identified as moral subjects in two dimensions. In the first dimension their action will be governed by orientation on the good life; in the second dimension they will subject the quest for socially binding norms to the 'moral perspective', seeking to ensure that the consequences and side-effects for the interests of each individual which result from the general pursuit of a norm can be recognized freely by all concerned.[5] The following reflections on globalization will be in keeping with such a conception. After taking the public gloss off the globalization debate I shall attempt a more precise account of globalization, where the international finance markets are becoming independent and the asymmetries of economic power are becoming more acute. The already existing areas where there is scope for political action need to be used and developed as a counter-force.

II. The demystification of globalization

Globalization became a fashionable word in the 1990s. The part of the debate on globalization which was prominent in public replaced the earlier debates on locations and was largely carried on from an ideological perspective: usually globalization had to serve as a cipher for interpreting the economic changes in the world after 1989. As a result it was used in an extremely inflationary and diffuse way. It could be used to denote the imperial expansion of the Western model of civilization into the so-called Third World, in the course of which traditional cultures disappear, the systems of a capitalist market economy and a formal democracy expand and the less developed economies are forcibly incorporated into the world market regime, dominated by the industrialized countries. The effects of this pressure towards globalization exerted by the industrial countries on the 'colonized' countries of the global economy of the south is also designated by this magic word, to denote a heightened pressure towards assimilation which newly industrialized threshold countries exert on individual business, branches and regions in industrial countries.

Often a 'fragmentation of society' is set against the 'globalization of the markets': a polarized development which was noted in newly industrialized countries of the Third World now also embraces mature industrial coun-

tries: social splits are becoming a global phenomenon accompanying economic growth.

Chronologically, the dating of the beginning of globalization is no less
diffuse. Some mark a turning point in 1971–73, when the fixed but adapt-
able currency rates were replaced by floating rates. Others put the divide
after the two oil price shocks of 1973 and 1980.[6] For many, the year 1989 is
an epoch-making turning point, whereas in the European countries and
especially in Germany the harshest post-war recession in 1993/94 is presented as the beginning of an unprecedented upheaval in the global market
and the global economy. Since the dating is so diffuse, the 'dramatic
impetus towards globalization' dissipates into a phantom, and globalization
proves to be a slow steady progress.[7]

How diffuse the perception of globalization has been in public is shown by
the titles of some best-sellers of the last decade.[8] Thus the debate on globalization supported by the media is predominantly about models of perception
and patterns of interpretation which can be detached from the reality
designated and begin to lead a life of their own. So it has become possible for
this debate to be taken over by monetarist propaganda orientated on supply.
Its three maxims are: Trust in the powers of the market to correct itself and
deregulate the labour market. The slim state is the best of all possible states,
so consolidate the state budget and privatize the public services. If the bank
of issue rigorously combats inflation, growth and employment will automatically rise, so leave the main economic responsibility to the bank. These
three maxims have been propagated with missionary zeal as the appropriate
answer to the 'pressure of globalization'.

The term 'system competition' shows the degree to which part of the
globalization debate has become the vehicle of the neo-classical dreamworld.
In this hypothesis economic competition as it exists in commodity and
finance markets is transferred to the state systems, say, of education, health,
old age insurance and the public infrastructure. The nation states are
allegedly competing for the sovereign decision of the economic subject in the
form of foreign traders or investors. The import of a commodity or a direct
investment abroad and the streams of commodities and the movements of
factors are interpreted as the demand for a public packet of taxes and benefits.[9] The question whether in the end the packets with the lowest social
standards, the least redistribution of commodities and a fallow infrastructure
of commerce survive as offers,[10] or whether the various preferences of the
customers enforce a colourful but always attractive spectrum of a legal and
social constitution with different combinations of public infrastructure and
its financing need not be pursued further. For the great elegance of the

model of economic subjects calculating in a sovereign way with individual packets of preferences, rational expectations and complete information, is diametrically opposed to its practical relevance. That countries compete with one another like businesses has to be termed an *idée fixe* which is not only wrong but dangerous, because it leads economic politics astray and provokes trade conflicts,[11] especially as the indicators of the competitiveness of a country are set in an extremely arbitrary way and cannot say very much.[12]

In order to strip globalization of its ideological character, it makes sense to spell out the term and to divide it into the four partial aspects of the international network of trade, direct foreign investments, the operation of transnational businesses and the international financial markets.[13] The role of information and communication techniques is usually overestimated,[14] whereas the migration of labour is largely limited to the global economy of the south, since the industrialized countries take effective precautions against such migration.

The scope of the international network of trade is not global. At most 30% of the global population are directly integrated into the global economy. Two-thirds of world trade remains within the three great trading blocks which formed at the end of the East-West confrontation. Germany handles two-thirds of the foreign trade with Western European industrial countries. The same can be said of direct foreign investments. Between 80% and 90% are made in developed industrialized countries to open up or safeguard markets.[15] However, the real international capital movements make up only 6% of global gross investments.[16] Certainly the transnational businesses are regarded as the motive force of globalization. They handle three-quarters of world trade; a third of world trade is trade within businesses, and this is tending to grow.

However, there are manifold forms of globalized production. Direct foreign investment is often the preliminary to or an element in multinational chains of value-creation. A globally integrated system of production presupposes that the components of homogeneous commodities and services supplied globally are made in different places and brought together. But there is good reason to relativize the weight of transnational businesses and their potential to threaten national governments. For they employ a mere 3% of the productive organized labour force worldwide.[17] Moreover they supplement their simulations, which are based on global integration, with components of regional identity.[18] Transnational businesses remain tied to their origin in countries with high wages; they continue to foster national traditions in the cultures in which they do business and aim to do business where they have a home base.

The international finance markets deserve the predicate 'global' in a real sense. The businesses in these markets have mushroomed. Even more rapid has been the rise in derivative financial businesses. Along with the growth in financial markets, between 1975 and 1985 the number of branches of foreign banks in the USA and Japan grew threefold in each case, and in Great Britain and Germany fourfold. But even the international financial markets are not as 'global', which they are often presented as being in the globalization debate. There are differences in the way in which the stock, bond, money and foreign currency markets are intertwined internationally; total intertwining would necessarily lead to a parity of real interest and to considerable disparities in national quotas of investment and savings. But this cannot be observed, though the connection between national savings and investment quotas became looser in the 1990s.[19] The money and foreign currency markets can be said to be 'thoroughly globalized', though not without the new information technologies as intermediaries.

The demystification of globalization and the specification of what can be understood by globalization do not justify any mood of alarm in the global economy of the north.[20] The most competitive countries internationally are at the same time countries with comfortable systems of social security and welfare.

III. Independence of the financial markets

Striking qualitative changes have been noted on the international finance markets since the middle of the 1970s and 1990s. They justify speaking of increasing networking and a concentration of businesses which span frontiers. The first striking change is the tendency for securities to take the place of bank credits. The stock markets are increasingly taking over the function of controlling businesses. Secondly, the privatization of risks on currency exchange can be noted, a consequence of the abolition of the Bretton Woods system. Here the futurization of financial business has intensified. Since information is exchanged globally about future risks, subjective expectations and value judgments are reflected in current currency movements

The transactions of the big institutional players like the pension funds contribute to a higher tendency to take risks by the owners of capital as soon as they can be certain that the International Monetary Fund and the central banks of the industrialized countries will collectively insure risky operations. There are signs that the international financial markets have detached themselves from the fundamental economic cycles. This can be seen in the fickleness of the stock exchanges and in speculative bubbles, in technological feedbacks, irrational reflexes of mood and collective infections, in the substantial shifts in exchange rates, for example of the German and US currency before 1999, which can hardly be explained in terms of real economics, and in speculative currency attacks like that against the Mexican currency at the beginning of 1995 and some of the South-East Asian currency in 1997, the more distant effects of which seriously shook Russia and Brazil. All this has a negative effect on investment, production, real income and consumption.[21]

This development massively unsettles planners in businesses which want to take long-term investment decisions and adopt new long-term positions that could relieve the labour market and the budgets of insurance schemes. Speculative gains and monopoly gains which can be produced by financial innovations become the indicators of expectations of yield on the financial markets. For the businesses, these in turn serve as a benchmark and rule for deciding on the profitability of an investment.

Waves of debt go with the globalized financial markets as water goes with the sea.[22] But the erection and demolition of the mountains of debt in the 1970s, 1980s and 1990s, the financial crises of the Asian countries of Thailand, Indonesia, the Philippines and South Korea in 1997, and the debt crises in Latin America have no comparable causes. The high involvement of the private economy, short-term capital debt and short-term capital outflow were the characteristics of the 'Asian crisis'. The 'fundamental' economies of these countries were thought to be sound. But the non-economic liberalization coincided with a credit boom on the international finance markets. The consequences of the financial crisis on the real economy were devastating: economic production fell by between 15% and 20%.

IV. Balances of power

Part of the debate on globalization is wrong at a central point about the processes and structures which really exist, in so far as it negligently leaves out of account the asymmetrical balances of power in world trade, transnational businesses and the international financial markets.

World trade does not predominantly follow the typical model of the international sharing of work which is explained by the comparative advantages of the cost and the relation of production factors of the countries integrated into the world market. It is largely governed by exchange relationships between mature industrial countries and within the same sectors. Alongside this, the polar relationship of dominant centres and dependent peripheries

goes a long way to explain the situation. World powers which have
dynamically growing economies, extensive internal markets, leading
currencies and a potential for military deterrence impose their political will
in regional alliances and international treaties and institutions. Thus north-
south trade and, parallel to it, direct investment in threshold countries also
stem from a colonial heritage and have military connotations. Or they
embody a current geo-strategic interest on the part of the leading powers.
The conditions under which the developing countries are integrated into
the global economy are formulated under the umbrella of the industrial
countries. The results of this 'power in exchange' are normally a regime of
trade in commodities which makes the developing country take the risk of
deteriorating exchange rates and a path towards industrialization involving
foreign debt and driven by devaluation.[23] Some industrial countries organize
their national economies with an offensive focus on exports and maintain
long-term trade surpluses which they refuse to reduce. By contrast, the
emergence of 'low wage economies', which are inappropriately made
responsible for high unemployment in mature industrial countries, primarily causes a problem of distribution. Structural change makes it possible
for all countries involved to increase their prosperity without automatically
guaranteeing fair distribution of the benefits of trade. When labour-
intensive production is farmed out and at the same time capital goods
are exported which have been produced with a high degree of technology, a
negative balance in some segments of the labour markets of mature industrial countries is unavoidable. Consequently the workers with few qualifica-
tions are among the losers in the structural change. Now appropriate
compensation for the losers could follow from this if the mature industrial
countries increased their efforts in branches of the economy intensive in
technology and capital, reduced their export burden and accelerated de-
industrialization. They could open up new markets in which personal
services were called for at home and provided for by small and medium-
sized businesses. A stronger internal orientation, which would be quite
natural for the European economic sphere, could help to adjust the distorted
balances of power in the global economy.

   The strong emphasis on transnational businesses in the global economy
has been followed by growing interest in a purely micro-economic analysis.
But precisely from this perspective it is necessary to make clearer distinctions. First, strategic alliances, co-operative agreements and participation
in domestic business or its (hostile) take-over are replacing a centralistic
direction of chains of production and value-creation. Secondly, the cost-
induced and procedure-orientated choice of location which involved the

shift of production to the so-called low-wage countries is being replaced by a preference for decentralized and differentiated business units near markets with great purchasing power, which lie in the global economic north. Thirdly, the centralization of the processes of decision-making is moving from the level of production to the level of the provision of services, namely research and development, finance and marketing. The concentration of such functions in an apparently virtual 'headquarters' transforms trans-national businesses into 'global players' which are in a position to limit quite considerably the internal sovereignty of individual, but not all, nation states over against their societies.[24] This change is accompanied by the use of evaluation systems, rating agencies and benchmarking procedures which have been developed in the USA; those who know how to use them can count themselves among the élite global leadership.[25] Such global players are displacing the concept which grew up in Germany after the Second World War that a business represents a personal alliance or contractual network of those who are personally and financially involved in it, namely the manager, staff, shareholders, banks, customers and suppliers. The business is exclusively understood as a resource in the hands of the shareholders. These can command a majority and appoint managers who are acceptable to them. They can cut out the profitable cores of businesses, and sell or scrap the rest, along with the staff.

The strident claim that the states are competing for mobile capital is probably meant to consolidate the superstition that the financial markets are the 'fifth force'[26] which controls state action. It is believed that the international finance markets make accessible authentic information about the potential of national economies and businesses and direct the streams of money and capital world-wide so that they are put to the best possible use. They are regarded as self-governing and embody a depoliticized economic efficiency. As incorruptible arbiters they reward correct political decisions and punish wrong ones. But under cover of the model world hoped for is hidden, first, the arrogant view that one can pass judgment on political goals from an Archimedean point which is defined in fiscal and monetary terms. Secondly, there is no indication that the international financial markets are shaped by the balances of power between the great institutional concerns, especially between the US-dominated pension funds and atomized small investors. The opportunities of gaining significant information, handing it on and exercising influence are divided asymmetrically. Even more important is the balance of power in the leading or anchor currencies and the non-convertible weak currencies. The banks of issue in the countries with leading currencies give absolute priority to the battle against inflation. The countries with dependent currencies are compelled to go along with what is now more headlong competition for a stable currency. To the degree that they disappoint the expectations of the rating agencies, they have to accept interest surcharges to compensate for the risk of devaluation. If they want to avoid deterring foreign direct investors, these countries have to accept a 'dollarization' (or a 'euroization'). So it is not automatically to be expected from the globalization of the financial markets that the level of prosperity and the quality of life in the peripheries of the global economy will be assimilated to that at its centres. Under the conditions of asymmetrical balances of power and exchange rates the disparity between them is made more acute, as also is the pressure of leading currencies on the countries dependent on them.

This pressure can also lead to a displacement of the German financial system which controls businesses through banks and credits and which makes long-term investment decisions possible through personal and financial networks. The US financial system controls businesses through the stock markets and especially through the pension funds. It compels managers to orientate their decisions primarily on the share prices of their business and to present the image of the business to the professional analysts in short-term periods. The domination of the US financial systems puts pressure on the welfare provisions of those involved in business in Germany, financed as part of the costs, because for those with monetary resources, private care covered by capital is more advantageous in times of high unemployment, lower investment and lesser rates of growth. Under the regime of the International Monetary Fund, countries with high levels of debt have programmes forced on them to ensure that they regain their creditworthiness and become attractive to foreign capital. That imports of capital are indispensable is justified by the existence of a 'savings gap', as if a capacity and a tendency to save governed the level and trend of investment. However, there are good reasons for assuming that the tendency of businesses to invest is driven by its expectations of turnover and profit; this means that the entrepreneurs get credit at the banks, hire staff, buy production capacity, produce, sell, and pay back the credits. Domestic saving is then the result of investment, state deficits and a surplus in the balance of trade. The key to a dynamic development lies in the creation of money and credit in the domestic banking sector, whereas the import of capital carries the risk of lasting trade deficits.[27]

V. No political impotence

Decision-makers with a democratic backing are not handed over impotently to world trade, transnational business and the international financial markets. The hypothesis that there is a vacuum in world politics is just not true. For the economic activities which go beyond frontiers were and largely are desired politically. And there are possibilities of political action within the framework of regional integration and international agreements.

In the sphere of European integration the potential threat of transnational businesses can be tamed if business councils, trade unions and supranational organs co-operate with one another. ASEAN or NAFTA have a similar purpose and mode of procedure to the EU. In Latin America the cohesion of MERCOSUR depends on a renunciation of hegemonial claims on the part of the big countries, on regional and social balances, on the consolidation of democracy and the participation of representatives of civil society.[28]

Moreover there are already numerous international treaties and institutions. However, the OECD, the International Monetary Fund, the World Bank and the World Trade Organization are dominated by the rich and powerful nations. The banks of issue in the leading industrial countries, whose finely balanced decisions are based on the Basle Committee of 1975, the Plaza Agreement of 1985, the Louvre Accord of 1987 and the Basle Agreement of 1988, have proved competent 'firemen', having intervened in favour of the Mexican currency and in favour of Asian currencies in order to prevent a collapse in the global financial system. In the future they could pay greater attention to the prevention of fires. The test case of their competence in financial policy will be the management of the so-called debt crisis and their contribution to an international financial architecture. The so-called Washington Consensus[29] is no longer normative for the crisis management of the 1990s but rather the 'post-Washington Consensus', for which the former President of the World Bank, Joseph Stiglitz, has campaigned: basic health care, basic education and public infrastructure must be given a stronger weighting in programmes of structural adaptation, and the legal rules must be reorganized.[30]

The foundations of a financial architecture favouring countries with a high level of debt that are mentioned in current discussion[31] are the Tobin tax, a tax on short-term financial transactions, controls on the movement of capital in developing countries, a stabilization of the exchange rates of leading currencies within a band, and above all an international law of insolvency: the debtor country is to be able to call on a comparative procedure leading to a decision which is orientated on its own capacities. The safeguarding of health, education and the environment are to have priority over the interests of creditors.

The organizations of the United Nations, including its subordinate organizations like UNESCO, UNIDO, UNICEF, WHO, FAO and ILO, can provide indirect democratic legitimation. The United Nations, which in the 1990s arranged five world summit conferences, has at any rate contributed towards the formation of a global public that is taking form in global agents in civil society like Amnesty International, Greenpeace, trade unions and the local churches. This development has been most marked in the greatest global social movement, the 'Jubilee 2000' campaign.[32] This initiative is an example of how transnational co-operation between those responsible for making state decisions, institutions and agents in civil society can be very effective.

Translated by John Bowden

Notes

*This article first appeared in German in the supplement to *Das Parlament*, 11 August 2000. It is reprinted with the kind permission of the author and publisher.

1. Niklas Luhmann, *Paradigm lost: Über die ethische Reflexion der Moral. Rede von Niklas Luhmann anlässlich der Verleihung des Hegel-Preises 1989*, Frankfurt am Main 1990, p. 41.

2. Cf. Max Weber, 'Politik als Beruf' in *Gesammelte Schriften*, Munich 1921, pp.369–450: 349–50; Siegfried F. Franke, 'Sozialdumping durch Schwellenländer?' in Hartmut Berg (ed), *Globalisierung der Wirtschaft. Formen – Konsequenzen*, Schriften des Vereins für Socialpolitik, NF 263, Berlin 1999, pp.157–82.

3. Cf. Karl Homann, 'Individualisierung: Verfall der Moral? Zum ökonomischen Fundament aller Moral' in *Aus Politik und Zeitgeschichte*, B21/97, pp.13–21.

4. Cf. Friedrich Hensbach, '"Globalisierung" aus wirtschaftsethischer Sicht' in *Aus Politik und Zeitgeschichte*, B 21/97, pp.3–12; id., *Beteiligt sein ist alles. Eine christliche Gesellschaftsethik*, Darmstadt 2000.

5. Cf. Jürgen Habermas, 'Diskursethik – Notizen zu einem Begründungsprogramm' in id., *Moralbewusstsein und kommunikatives Handeln*, Frankfurt am Main ³1989, pp.75f.

6. Cf. the Lisbon Group, *Grenzen des Wettbewerbs. Die Globalisierung der Wirtschaft und die Zukunft der Menschheit*, Munich 1997, p.48.

7. Cf. Christoph F. Büchtemann and Ulf-Wilhelm Kuhlmann, 'Internationalisierungsstrategien deutscher Unternehmen: Am Beispiel von Mercedes-Benz'

in Pamela Meil (ed), *Globalisierung industrielle Produktion*, Frankfurt am Main and New York 1996, pp.60–3.

8. Cf. Hans-Peter Martin and Harald Schumann, *Die Globalisierungsfalle*, Reinbek 1996; Elmar Altvater and Birgit Mahnkopf, *Grenzen der Globalisierung*, Münster 1997; Kurt Hübner, *Der Globalisierungskomplex*, Berlin 1998; Daniel Cohen, *Fehldiagnose Globalisierung*, Frankfurt am Main 1998; Wissenschaftliche Arbeitsgruppe für weltkirchliche Aufgaben der Deutschen Bischofkonferenz (ed), *Die vielen Gesichter der Globalisierung*, Bonn 1999; Ulrich Steger, *Globalisierung gestalten*, Berlin etc. 1999.

9. Cf. Theresia Theurl, 'Globalisierung als Selektionsprozess ordnungspolitischer Paradigmen' in H. Berg (ed), *Globalisierung der Wirtschaft* (n.2), pp.33–40.

10. Cf. Hans-Werner Sinn, 'The Limits to Competition Between Economic Regimes', *Empirica, Austrian Economic Papers* 17, 1990, pp.3–14.

11. Cf. Paul Krugman, 'Wettbewerbsfähigkeit: Eine gefährliche Wahnvorstellung' in Werner Fricke (ed), *Zukunft der Industriegesellschaft, Jahrbuch Arbeit und Technik*, Bonn 1996, pp.37–49.

12. Cf. Hartmut Küchle, 'Zur Messung der Wettbewerbsfähigkeit von Volkswirtschaften' in WSI-Mitteilungen 47, 1994, pp.180–90; Renate Ohr, 'Internationale Wettbewerbsfähigkeit einer Volkswirtschft. Zur Aussagefähigkeit ausgewählter Indikatoren' in H. Berg, *Globalisierung der Wirtschaft* (n.2), pp.51–67.

13. Cf. Hartmut Küchle, 'Deutschlands Position auf dem Weltmarkt', *WSI-Mitteilungen* 49, 1996, pp.295–303.

14. Cf. Kai Hafez, 'Medien-Kommunkation-Kultur: Irrwege und Perspektiven der Globalisierungsdebatte' in Rainer Tetzlaff (ed), *Weltkulturen unter Globalisierungsdruck*, Bonn 2000, pp.93–117.

15. Cf. Kurt Hübner, *Die Globalisierungskomplex: grenzenlöse Ökonomie – grenzenlose Politik?*, Berlin 1998.

16. Cf. Horst Siebert, 'Disziplinierung der nationalen Wirtschaftspolitik durch die internationale Kapitalmobilität' in Dieter Duwendag (ed), *Finanzmärkte im Spannungsfeld von Globalisierung, Regulierung und Geldpolitik*, Berlin 1998, p.43.

17. Cf. Hans-Erich Müller, 'Heimatlose Weltbürger?, *Die Mitbestimmung* 43, 1997, pp.34–7.

18. Cf. Herbert A. Henzler, 'Die Globalisierung von Unternehmen im internationalen Vergleich', *Zeitschrift für Betriebswirtschaft, Ergänzunsheft* 2, 1992, pp.83–97.

19. Cf. Horst Gischer, 'Kapitalmarktintegration, Zinsvolatilität und gewerbliche Kreditnachfrage' in H. Berg, *Globalisierung der Wirtschaft* (n.2), pp.183–206; Martin Feldstein and Charles Horioka, 'Domestic Saving and International Capital Flows', *Economic Journal* 90, June 1980, pp.314–29; H. Siebert, 'Disziplinierung der nationalen Wirtschaftspolitik' (n.16), p.42.

20. Cf. Theresia Theurl, 'Globalisierung als Selektionsprozess ordnungspoliti-

scher Paradigmen' in H. Berg (ed), *Globalisierung der Wirtschaft* (n.2), pp.33–40.

21. Cf. Hansjörg Herr, *Geld, Währungswettbewerb und Währungssysteme. Theoretische und historische Analyse der internationalen Geldwirtschaft*, Frankfurt am Main 1992; Manfred Nitsch, 'Vom Nutzen des monetär-keynsianischen Ansatzes für Entwicklungstheorie und -politik' in Renate Schubert (ed), *Neue Wachstums- und Aussenhandelstheorie. Implikationen für die Entwicklungstheorie und -politik*, Schriften des Vereins fur Socialpolitik, NF Band 269, Berlin 1999, pp.183–214.

22. Cf. id., 'Finanzströme und Verschuldung' in Stiftung Entwicklung und Frieden (eds), *Global Trends 2000*, Frankfurt am Main 1999, pp.219–43.

23. Cf. Hartmut Elsenhans, 'Globalisierung intensivieren: Chance der Südens und des Westens' in Reimut Jochimsen (ed), *Globaler Wettbewerb und weltwirtschaftliche Ordnungspolitik*, Bonn 2000, pp.74–7.

24. Cf. Wolfgang H. Reinicke, 'Globale Ordnungspolitik: Gedanken zu einem überfälligen Thema' in Ullrich Heilmann, Dietmar Kath and Norbert Kloten (eds), *Entgrenzung als Erkenntnis- und Gestaltungsaufgabe*, Berlin 1998, pp.285–98.

25. Cf. Ewald Nowotny, 'Der Machtfactor multinationaler Unternehmen und ihre Funktion im globalen Wettbewerb' in R. Jochimsen, *Globaler Wettbewerb* (n.23), pp.253–88.

26. Rolf-E. Breuer, 'Die fünfte Gewalt', *Die Zeit*, 27 April 2000, pp.21f.

27. Cf. Friedhelm Hensbach and Bernhard Emunds (eds), *Finanzströme in Entwicklungsländer – in welcher Form zu wessen Vorteil*, Frankfurt am Main 2000; Elmar Altvater, 'Monopoly spielen oder Mut machen', *Frankfurter Rundschau*, 11 September 2000, p.9.

28. Cf. Wolfram Klein, *Der Mercosur. Wirtschaftliche Integration, Unternehmer und Gewerkschaften*, Freiburg 1996; Hartmut Sangmeister, *Mercosur: Möglichkeiten und Grenzen der Integration*, Heidelberg 1996.

29. Cf. Reiner Falk, 'Die systemgerechte Verarbeitung von Schuldenkrisen' in *Weltwirtschaft, Ökologie und Entwicklung*, WEED (ed), *Schuldenreport 1999*, p.26.

30. Cf. Joseph E. Stiglitz, 'More Instruments and Broader Goals. Moving toward the Post-Washington Consensus' in Gudrun Kochendörfer-Lucius and Boris Pleskovic (eds), *Development Issues in the Twenty-First Century*, Viall Borsig Workshop Series 1998, Berlin and Washington DC, pp.11–39.

31. Cf. Andreas Hauskrecht, 'Anforderung an eine Weltfinanzordnung in einer globalisierten Welt' in R. Jochimsen, *Globaler Wettbewerb* (n.23), pp.98–123.

32. Cf. Barbara Unmüssig, 'Die HIPC-Initiative. Kein Durchbruch für die hochverschuldeten armen Länder' in *Schuldenreport 1999* (n.29), p.26.

The Global Ethic Project:
A Challenge for Education

JOHANNES LÄHNEMANN

In a village in south-west Scotland a primary school teacher is giving her children some first ideas about different religions. To liven up the lesson she has produced an exercise book. It has the title 'Houses without Bedrooms' and contains pictures and sketches of religious buildings: church, mosque, synagogue, Hindu temple. Like the teacher, all the pupils belong to the Church of Scotland. When the elders ask the teacher why she is discussing something so exotic as strange religions with the children, she replies: 'You and your children live in the country. You go shopping once a week in the supermarket. Your children don't need to use money. But you think it important for us also to teach children in school how to use money. They will certainly need to use money in their future life. It's just the same with the different religions. They will be part of the future world in which your children live and the children must know something about them, even if they don't encounter them yet.'

This example, which we heard in discussions about religious education in Great Britain,[1] indicates the importance of the ideas for educational work down to primary and elementary level and in villages which culturally seem to be homogeneous, which are associated with the Global Ethic Project and the Global Ethic Declaration. This challenge will be developed here in ten theses. They start from important perspectives which arose at the Fifth Nuremberg Forum 'The Global Ethic Project in Education',[2] but also relate to the more recent developments which have been sponsored above all by the Global Ethic Foundation.

I. Effort in education

The maxims formulated by Hans Küng,

- No peace among the nations without peace among the religions
- No peace among the religions without dialogue between the religions

- No dialogue between the religions without research into the foundation of the religions[3]

can be supplemented as follows:

No peace, no dialogue and no work on the foundations of the religions without effort in education.

Here is an important field for testing the idea of a global ethic, a sphere where it becomes evident whether the Global Ethic Project can be made specific. As an initial insight we can say that only if members of the rising generation have respect for their fellow human beings, feel responsibility for all creation, animate and inanimate, and are sensitive to hatred, violence and all developments which are hostile to life and society, will they be equipped for a life in community which opens up a future for our planet.

The future of our 'spaceship earth' will also depend decisively on whether the generations to come – the children and the young people now alive, and those who will be born in the next years – are in a position to shape this future in a responsible way.[4]

The frameworks for this are as varied as can be imagined in the various regions and countries of the world. The spectrum extends from countries with highly developed educational systems in which the religious and ethical dimension is also consistently incorporated into the curricula of schools and colleges, through countries in which the educational system is one-sidedly related to the economy, through 'threshold countries' in which great educational efforts are being made but which cannot keep pace with the population growth, to those which almost completely lack any economic basis for the development of an educational system.

Here detrimental phenomena can be made out, and not only in the poor countries, in which often child labour, child slavery, child prostitution and life as 'street children' affects many adolescents. Even in the highly-industrialized nations, children are abandoned, young people are neglected, become drug users and are ready to use violence, and at many points put excessive demands on parents and teachers. An important educational starting point for a reorientation is the development of inter-cultural education, which from tentative approaches at what is more the level of folklore has developed into a multi-faceted discipline with marked relevance to practice. Without the work of encounter and sensitizing which is done here, the variety of initiatives against xenophobia and the predominantly successful steps taken in integrating foreign children into our schools and educational institutions outside school are inconceivable.[5]

However, in the face of the current global challenges, a global framework can also be sketched which can follow contours that have already been mapped by the Global Ethic Foundation. It involves:

- learning for a *habitable earth* (in the face of the threat of ecological collapse);
- learning for a *mature perception* of the freedoms and responsibilities which accrue to the individual in accordance with human rights (in the face of the threat of enslavement to technocratic systems, simplistic ideologies, impoverishment, and economic and political slavery and criminalization);
- learning for a *meaningful way of shaping life* (in the face of the threat of being 'taken over' by the media culture and the ideology of prosperity, and the 'environmental pollution of the soul');
- learning for *co-existence in solidarity*, in families and communities against regional and international horizons (in the face of the dangers of disintegrating family structures, the lack of an elementary awareness of ethical values and the revival of national fanaticisms and particularisms).[6]

II. Responsible systems of meaning

Educational effort along the lines of the global ethic is inspired by the view that there are religions and world-views as 'responsible systems of meaning' which are in a position to communicate their traditions of values to the present pluralistic reality. They do not need to be made uniform but to be specified, so that they can give meaning to life and inspire responsible action from their particular tradition – with its spirituality, its foundations for knowledge, its social and ethical formation.

'Responsible systems of meaning' are essential in the face of the pluralization of the forms and circumstances of life which go with a more marked individualization. In the freedom of world-view within which we all live and can develop, almost everyone can compile his or her own pick-and-choose religion and world-view. Here the main motifs can be related to the self: the sense of responsibility to the whole of society which distinguishes the great religious traditions can easily be pushed aside. On the other hand, people can be 'taken over' by the global market of media, advertising and consumerism: what 'one' has to have, what 'one' has to possess, how 'one' has to behave (e.g. the take-over of the culture of eating by the world-wide fast food chains; Dallas in more than eighty countries; the take-over of the sexual behaviour of young people by *Bravo* magazine).

By contrast, the great religious traditions represent a combination of faith, insights, doctrines and rites which can be a basis for life, a social structure, and ethics which give individuals their place in relation to the community and put them in an inalienable context of responsibility. I need not enlarge here on how constricting these systems could and can be, how they attach strings to people and limit their development as well as providing support and security. Emancipation from the tutelage of religion and world-views is a process which has been long and painful, and many societies are still caught up in it.

The danger in emancipation from the value-systems which have been handed down lies in the randomness of values, in which egotistic quasi-religions like consumerism can spread. Here there is no meaningful way back to the uniformity of a dogmatic confession. Here the task which is relevant to education is rather to bring the religious traditions up to date in dialogue with the modern history of freedom,[7] and in so doing take into account the totality of the global challenges. Here, despite all the differences, convergences between the religious traditions can be discovered without one's having to give up the specific features of one's own tradition.

The 'advantage' of the religions over non-religious world-views, which should not in any way be disparaged, is that they can live by a *religio*, a binding back to a basic meaning of existence, by spiritual sources which transcend finitude and can give support and strength even in the face of human limits. An urgent and manifold field of tasks awaits in respect of the theological and ethical inspirations which could result from dialogue between the religions.

III. Structural conditions

Education along the lines of the global ethic depends on structural conditions: that children experience love, security and protection; that possibilities are offered to them of living, learning and developing with personal support from others:
- *free from exploitation in structures of impoverishment*
- *free from neglect in structures of consumerism.*

Work on the improvement of structural conditions must be understood as a political priority to which the religious and ideological communities have to make their contribution.

Time and again it becomes evident that children in warlike conflicts, in unjust social structures, in family conflicts and in their dependence on educational possibilities are among the weakest and most easily neglected members of society. Necessary though the rising generation is for the ongoing existence and development of the earth, it is structurally weak as part of society. For all the efforts in the ecological sphere, in peace studies, in the commitment to more justice and in all the schemes of a meaningful future, at the same time there is also a need to think in educational terms. How can children become participants in this process? Their participation is as it were the acid test for the transformation of structures.

Here the same ways need not be taken everywhere. Where structures of impoverishment predominate, the beginning needs to be different from where a neglect through consumerism threatens. The essential thing is work which enables the basic needs of children to be supplied in the particular context in which they live: love, security, protection, opportunities to live, learn and develop with personal support. In other words, where children are forced to work as child labour if they are to be able to live and survive at all, an elementary humanization of their living conditions must stand in the foreground, along with a minimum of school education or at least literacy training, so that they are not cut off from any possibility of coming of age and acting on their own responsibility. Where the traumas of war have to be coped with, practice in the morality of living and learning will be a central task. Where children tend to be neglected in the big cities of Europe, education in leisure is an essential task, and school and living space need to be brought closer together.

In all these contexts the aspect of 'personal support' is important; in other words, the reinforcement and support of structures of family responsibility requires corresponding economic and social frameworks. Here the emphasis can no longer be put on the 'whole' family, welcome as this framework must continue to be. It is crucial for children to grow up within a structure of trustworthy relationships in which they do not need to feel left alone. At our forum, Friedhelm Zubke spoke of 'ethical parenthood', which is not limited to the physical father and the physical mother.[8] In my view the SOS children's villages, which offer otherwise solitary children precisely such family structures, set a good example here.

The Christian schools in the Near East, in which children of different confessions are brought up together and taught to respect one another, are another example. They include the Johann Ludwig Schneller school in Khirbet Kanafar in Lebanon, in which many war orphans of the different groups involved in the civil war were brought up through all those war years in a spirit of understanding and toleration.[9]

The state initiatives here depend on the involvement of communities with a religious and humanitarian stamp, just as in turn these need support and encouragement from the state and society.[10]

IV. Human rights and communication

Education effort along the lines of the global ethic is a differentiated education in values. For its implementation it needs to be based on a realization of human rights and to communicate with the traditions of religions and world views which influence society.

It is presupposed here that education in values has to be one of the main tasks of education. Without orientation in questions of meaning, value and ethics, the means for a responsible coming of age are lacking. That also means that questions of meaning, value and ethics in connection with a world–view and in particular a religious tradition represent a genuine realm of tasks for school education which is best fulfilled by an independent school discipline, without relieving the other school disciplines and out-of-school education of their tasks. But this is a sphere of tasks which calls for specific professional competence in religious and ethical questions of a kind that in my view cannot be introduced in passing by teachers of history, geography and the social sciences.

That is why religious instruction is so important. It has the task of providing aids for orientation, existence and action in the light of the religious traditions which particularly determine our history and in respect of the present ideological and religious challenges to a pluralistic society.

It is essential that religious education which is related to a confession or co-operates with a confession should make adolescents familiar with the roots of their own tradition and culture as a 'system of meaning which is capable of responsibility'.[11] There can hardly be a serious encounter with other value traditions without such a basic orientation. However, the communication with such a religious tradition must prove itself to be capable of dialogue in the state school, in conversation between the disciplines and in the life of a pluralistic democratic society. Such teaching has a decisive 'preventative' task in the face of religions and world–views which on the one hand can result in uncritical adaptation to the ideals of consumerism and on the other can easily be misused for ethnic-religious fantasies, as we have been shown by the example of former Yugoslavia. Religious education or a corresponding alternative discipline is at present also provided for as a subject in the schools of all European states with the exception of France (apart from Alsace-Lorraine), and usually in the former Eastern bloc states.

However, in many places there is no infrastructure which is to any degree adequate in the sphere of guidelines and the development of textbooks, school organization and especially the training of teachers. Many of the difficulties can be illustrated from the introduction of religious education in the former East German states and the problems which face the development of Muslim religious education for the roughly 700,000 Muslim pupils in the West German states and Berlin.[12]

V. Non-violent resolution of conflicts

Educational effort along the lines of the global ethic is education towards the non-violent resolution of conflicts.

The basic problem here is that the view that violent action is rewarding, that the stronger win through, and that using one's elbows leads to success, is confirmed time and again by practical experience and is reinforced in the media. In regions of conflict like Israel/Palestine, Lebanon or former Yugoslavia, children have been confronted with the use of force in everyday life to such a degree that they can hardly imagine people living together without the use of violence. Among us school heads and teachers complain about instances of the use of force among children, in which wherever fights break out they can boil over into what virtually amounts to the torture of the losers. A big advertisement for the German Investment Trust (DIT) uses photographs of the managers as children, showing them with boxing gloves on. Already as children they have learned to land the right blows!

In the religions, which for a long time have regarded war and the use of violence as unavoidable and quite often have sanctioned it theologically, there is a line of rethinking which is relevant to education and which still needs to be worked out far more systematically than before: beginning with the peace churches of the Quakers, Mennonites and Methodists, through the unique example of Mahatma Gandhi and Martin Luther King, who as a Christian learned from the Hindu Gandhi, to the peace and civil rights movements of the last two decades, which have moved more people than could ever have been imagined previously in history. The examples from the revolution in East Germany, the efforts at reconciliation after the end of apartheid in South Africa inspired by Nelson Mandela, or the commitment to dialogue and peace built up by Prince Hassan bin Talal of the Jordanian royal family are to be set against the excess of reports of violence in the media.

Here too it is necessary to relate educational efforts quite specifically to the particular context: much can be learned from efforts in parallel contexts.

As a convincing example of this I want to mention the peace school in Neve Shalom/Wahat al-Salam near Jerusalem.[13] In this village shared by

Jews and Palestinians, both young and adult Jews and Palestinians are brought together in encounter seminars in order to work towards breaking down fear and mistrust and building up mutual trust. The seminars, in which people from the two sides are often directly together for the first time, are characterized by three phases: a first phase in which they meet cautiously and courteously and avoid controversy; a second phase in which the real anxieties and reservations, hurts and humiliations (particularly experienced on the Palestinian side) come to view and are often expressed very aggressively – enough time must be allowed for this phase; and a third phase in which people begin to understand the other side, their picture of the historical, political, economic and not least religious factors becomes more differentiated, a new sensitivity develops, and relationships and often enough friendships are built up over the divides. More than 20,000 young people and adults have so far taken part in these meetings. Groups from Israel and abroad visit Neve Shalom/Wahat al-Salam. Many groups in the peace movement use the models developed by the school.

This example can easily be related to the aims of the Association for Peace Education in Tübingen which Hans Küng introduced at the end of his lecture to the Nuremberg Forum:

- Learning to sustain a global order in which respect for human dignity come first
- Learning to empathize with others
- Learning to express feelings and to discuss them in dialogue with one's opposite number
- Learning to resolve conflicts constructively and to deal with aggression in a non-violent way
- Making room for action on one's own responsibility
- Setting credible examples and orientating oneself on them[14]

It is a task for the future to work out and experiment with training and behavioural programmes for non-violent action (se e.g. the model of Marshall Rosenberg in the USA) for the different educational contexts.

VI. Comprehensive respect for life

Educational effort along the lines of a global ethic is education for comprehensive respect for life.

I need not offer here an analysis of how the foundations of our existence are threatened by a possible ecological collapse, since the threat has been demonstrated to us often enough. The challenge here is so great that we simply cannot go on engaging in ethnic and religious conflicts with all their squandering of power and resources.

Here, by way of example, as a specialist in religious education I simply want to sketch out the approach which Christian theology and religious education has arrived at in our generation. Over against an interpretation of the command to human beings to dominate the earth which appears in Genesis 1 and is hostile to the environment and ultimately hostile to life, it has discovered the line of building up and preserving, of joy at creation and praise of creation – as this appears in the Psalms (Ps.104), in the images and parables of the preaching of Jesus, or in hymns. In the new curriculum for Protestant religious education in primary schools in Bavaria the topic is deliberately built up in lessons between the first and third years.[15] The theme of the first year is 'Discovering God's Good Creation': the pupils are to be led to joy and gratitude for all creation by observing the beauty and variety of life, growth and blossoming in the environment. The theme in the second year is 'Discovering Ordinances of Preservation in Creation', by dealing with the story of Noah and the Flood; that in the third year is 'Praising God's Good Creation', in connection with the fine images of Ps.104. Suggested activities are: for the first year arranging a patch of wild flowers in a corner of the school premises and for the third year devising a service in praise of creation.[16]

In his lecture to the Fifth Nuremberg Forum, Karl-Josef Kuschel showed us how in the theology of Genesis the monotheistic religions can listen to one another and learn with one another.[17] They must also do so out of new respect for the traditions of the nature religions, to which Geiko Müller-Fahrenholz has drawn our attention; indeed these have shown a quite different sensitivity to non-human life.[18]

The speech by Chief Seattle to the President of the United States about the earth that one cannot buy may first have been composed in our century, but it is nevertheless very impressive. That it has found an echo in religious education in Germany indicates a line of inter-religious dialogue for Christian religious teaching. This line must be developed into a form of teaching in our schools which is inter-disciplinary – and that is an educational task for the future. Here too we cannot afford to neglect the professional competence of neighbouring disciplines.[19]

VII. Truthfulness – tolerance – mutual respect

Educational effort along the lines of a global ethic is education for truthfulness, tolerance and mutual respect.

The Global Ethic Declaration has paid particular attention to this area. For in it the religions, and religious and inter-religious education, are quite specially challenged. Not only has the deliberate and unconscious disparagement of those of other faiths (usually without any well-founded knowledge of their belief) done terrible damage in history, but often enough even today politics is carried on with sheer ignorance, deliberate distortion and disinformation, and thus demarcation and defamation are practised specifically also in the religious sphere.

The undifferentiated view of Islam as a power which threatens the West and the whole world that is promoted in broadcasts by groups like the so-called Christian Centre – supported by a media market which started from Communism as a hostile stereotype – is an example of this, as conversely is the fact that in Cairo a university lecture can be announced under the title 'Why there are no values in the West'. Those who know, those who have differentiated knowledge, those who have learned to investigate and ask questions cannot simply be lied to and have the wool pulled over their eyes.

Here in particular the religions and religious education have a necessary task of orientation and encounter which is based on a differentiated dialogue between the religions. The important thing is to prepare adolescents for a co-existence which is not burdened by barriers of prejudice, but in which, rather, it is possible to listen to one another and learn from one another; which leads to the breaking down of barriers and the widening of horizons on all sides.

At the Fourth Nuremberg Forum in 1991 I presented a survey of the guidelines, the textbooks and the training of teachers in European countries; this has still not been superseded. It showed that over the last twenty years – especially in Western and Northern Europe – more has been done than ever before in history about religious and cultural encounter, but that this nevertheless still remains quite inadequate in the educational field generally. The work of the Shap Working Party on World Religions in Education in Great Britain would be a positive example, as in Germany would be the Cologne school book project on the treatment of Islam, first in German and then also in other European school books. Both examples show that it is possible to identify and criticize prejudice and that it is possible to learn to get to know and understand the faith of others as it appears to them.

The basic principle here is practice in a change of perspective, 'stepping into the shoes of others'. Manfred Schreiner, Director of Schools in Nuremberg, has shown quite practical ways with his 'models of teaching against racism and xenophobia':[20] here all at once foreign children become subjects instead of objects, who for example can help with explanations on visits to a mosque. Then a pupil exchange is arranged in which German children spend a weekend with a foreign family and vice versa. Shared involvement is brought about by partnership with children in a crisis area of the world about which information is given in school and for which aid material is organized. This example already points to the sphere of tasks which is addressed in the eighth thesis.

The problem here is the isolation of such efforts, which is only slowly being overcome; there is little international research in the area and so far these issues have not satisfactorily been transformed into teacher education, especially when it comes to a knowledge and understanding of other cultures and religions.

VIII. Solidarity against international horizons

Educational effort along the lines of a global ethic is education for life in solidarity in families and communities against regional and international horizons.

As constraints in this extraordinarily wide field of tasks I have already mentioned on the one hand the restricted possibilities of life and development among children in many poor countries which are torn with conflicts and on the other the images of a prosperous society which conflict with a far-reaching solidarity.

Education is not all-powerful in the face of these structures. But it is not impotent either. In a fundamental article, Hans Karl Beckmann has sketched out the contours of a realistic educational approach which can make its distinctive and indispensable contribution in combatting the tendencies which destroy solidarity and can show support for those with whom there needs to be solidarity.[21]

In the area of theme 5 of the Forum, in which conceptions and models for work in communities and families are presented, there are encouraging examples for education for co-existence in solidarity from countries like India and Sri Lanka, as well as from Germany. A. T. Ariyaratne, who can with some justification be called the Gandhi of Sri Lanka, describes the principles and praxis of the Sarvodaya = 'Prosperity for All' movement. With educational work, rural and craft development with the simplest means, medical work and work on human rights, this movement is active in more than 15,000 villages of the island, which is shaken with religious and ethnic crises.[22] Its basis is a community ethic derived from Buddhism which embraces human beings and nature: it includes spiritual renewal, self-improvement, and practical steps towards satisfying basic needs with few means. The small manageable communities, which in Ariyaratne's view could also be formed in cities, aimed at bringing the responsibility of the individual to bear in the face of all schematically globalistic attempts at a solution, are essential for the success of this work, which is attacked time and again by the main parties precisely because of its character of reconciliation which transcends the religions.

One community-related model from Germany has been introduced by Klaus Kürzdörfer; this is the 'Ark project', a suburban project from Kiel which is carried out every year.[23] The fact that representatives of twenty-one nations and individuals from many religious and non-religious traditions live together calls for inter-cultural and inter-religious perspectives to oppose hostility and segregation: here the ark becomes the symbol of the deliverance of the world and life, in connection with the different religious traditions in which it has its place. It is important that in this one-week project with children space is made for the self-development of the different modes of faith (including the pastors and the imams). Successful examples of the practice of solidarity are educationally effective in the best sense, on both a small and a large scale: they prevent apathy and can prove inviting and infectious. A systematic documentation and networking of them can provide a basis for the Global Ethic Project.

That brings me to the last two theses, in which I want to direct attention to the future and to necessary tasks which have already been indicated in the previous theses.

IX. Educational work

Educational effort along the lines of a global ethic needs educational work — especially in the areas of conflict education, environmental education, religious, inter-religious and inter-cultural education.

Each of the areas of education mentioned at the same time denotes spheres of research. Here the first task is the necessary research into the conditions of conflictual behaviour, attitudes to the environment, and communal religious and social life. Here educational work is not merely an applied science in which the scholarly results or ideal principles are implemented. Rather, it is a systematic, mediating discipline.

I have already mentioned particular demands in connection with the specific sphere of religious and inter-religious education: here the first demand is the improvement of the infrastructure in the schools and – centrally – in the training of teachers. Religious studies must take its place alongside theology as a further discipline in the training of teachers of religion, a requirement to which even the highly developed German system of training teachers does justice only at a few places. Moreover there is an urgent demand for qualified training of teachers of ethics and teachers of Islam who will be in a position to give Islamic religious education in Germany. Elementary knowledge of religious and cultural traditions which are relevant for our schools must also be part of the canon of teacher training. Work on guidelines and research for school books also needs to be broader and deeper. Now at last the Cologne school-book project on Islam has been given a counterpart: the investigation of the depiction of Christianity in school books in countries stamped by Islam.[24]

So more than enough tasks are waiting. And we need a many-sided collaboration to be able to do more justice to them than previously.[25]

X. International co-operation

Educational effort along the lines of a global ethic needs co-operation, international exchange and reciprocal inspiration through the documentation and evaluation of existing educational projects and the stimulation and development of new ones.

I think that this thesis is obvious: even in our closer environment the situation in schools, which has often become difficult, can only be coped with co-operatively. Where there is no exchange between teachers, where they hide their problems from one another, the burn-out syndrome and a premature retirement from professional life are pre-programmed. Where teachers and other educationalists are open and are given support and training, even difficult crisis situations can often be coped with.

In our forums the fruitfulness of mutual inspiration has also been confirmed within an international framework: with for example the ideas about imaginative learning presented by Reijo Heinonen from Finland;[26] with the perspective of a collaboration in education by Christians, Jews and Muslims in the Near East which Mitri Raheb from Bethlehem has sketched out;[27] or with the principles for the rebuilding of religious and ethical education in the schools of South Africa which has been developed by Gordon Mitchell.[28] In his Habilitationsschrift, Johannes Rehm evaluates the ongoing projects in the key multi-cultural regions and from the perspective of the global ethic connects them with European experiences and conceptions.

At international conferences there is on the one hand time and again amazement at how many forward-looking projects and initiatives there are, and on the other amazement at how little people know about what each other is doing.

Consequently the task of the Peace Education Standing Commission set up by the World Conference on Religion and Peace is particularly important. It is the documentation and evaluation of existing educational projects and the stimulation and development of new ones. Günther Gebhardt has done preliminary work here, and in his dissertation has presented a first systematic investigation of peace education in the religious peace movements.[29]

Just as in Great Britain, for example, there is an Interfaith Network in which all inter-religious activities in the United Kingdom have a focal point, so there should be a network for international inter-religious education on peace and a global ethic. However, much support from both heaven and earth is still needed here if we are to find additional strength from those in education, religion and ethics who are usually already overstretched, and to raise the basic finance neeeded.

Translated by John Bowden

Notes

1. Taken from J. Lähnemann, *Evangelische Religionspädagogik in interreligiöse Perspektive*, Göttingen 1998, p.13.
2. J. Lähnemann (ed), *Das Projekt Weltethos in der Erziehung. Referate und Ergebnisse des Nürnberger Forums 1994*, Hamburg 1995 = Pädagogische Beitrage zur Kulturbegegnung 14. The theses were first published in 'Weltethos und Erziehungspraxis – 10 Thesen' in H. Küng and K.-J. Kuschel (eds), *Wissenschaft und Weltethos*, Munich 1998, pp.217–38.
3. Most recently in Global Ethic Foundation, Waldhäuser Strasse 23, D 72076 Tübingen, October 1995.
4. For this and what follows see J. Lähnemann, 'Das "Projekt Weltethos" und die Aufgabe der Erziehung' in J. Rehm (ed), *Verantwortlich leben in der Weltgemeinschaft. Zur Auseinandersetzungen des 'Projekt Weltethos'*, Munich 1994, pp.68–71: 68f.
5. However, the inter-religious perspective has been marginalized too long in

inter-cultural education. On this see J. Lähnemann (ed), *Interreligiöse Erziehung 2000. Die Zukunft der Religions- und Kulturbegegnung. Referate und Ergebnisse des Nürnberger Forums 1997*, Hamburg 1998 = Pädagogische Beiträge zur Kulturbegegnung 16.

6. J. Lähnemann, 'Evangelische Erziehung vor globalen Herausforderungen' in id., *Weltethos in der Erziehung*, pp.221–9: 222.

7. This starting point was already developed in religious education in 1975 by Karl Ernst Nipkow, *Grundfragen der Religionspädagogik 1, Gesellschaftliche Herausforderungen und theoretische Ausgangspunkte*, Gütersloh 1975, see esp. p.173.

8. F. Zubke, 'Prinzip Ethik als tragende Kategorie von Elternschaft' in Lähnemann, *Weltethos in der Erziehung*, pp.372–81.

9. Najim Haddad, 'Kinderschicksale und Erziehungsverantwortung in religiös-politisch fanatisiertem Umfeld – Christliche Schulen im Nahe Osten' in J. Lähnemann (ed), *Das Wiedererwachen der Religionen als pädagogische Herausforderung. Interreligiöse Erziehung im Spannungsfeld von Fundamentalismus und Säkularismus*, Hamburg 1992 = Padagogische Beiträge zur Kulturbegegnung 10, pp.313–21; U. Kadelbach, 'Christliche Schulen im Nahe Osten – Orte der Friedenserziehung' in J. Lähnemann (ed), *Weltreligionen und Friedenserziehung. Wege zur Toleranz. Schwerpunkt:Christentum-Islam*, Hamburg 1989 = Pädagogische Beiträge zur Kulturbegegnung 7, pp.248–59.

10. This field of peace research in the broader sense is being worked on e.g. by the Peace Education Standing Commission (PESC) of Religions for Peace/World Conference on Religion and Peace (WCRP). The results of the work are now available in *Peace Education from Faith Traditions*, produced by Lehrstuhl für Evangelischen Religionspädagogik, Regensburger Strasse 160, D 90478 Nürnberg, 2001 (website under www.wcrp.de/pesc/). This publication also introduces the educational work of the Global Ethic Foundation: G. Gebhardt, 'Education Toward a Global Ethic. Educational Activities in the Framework of the Global Ethic Project', ibid., pp.42f.

11. See J. Lähnemann, 'Zielsetzungen und Aufgabenstellungen eines modernen evangelischen Religionsunterrichts in einer pluralen Gesellschaft' in M. Liedke (ed), *Religiöse Erziehung und Religionsunterricht*, Bad Heilbrunn 1994, pp.307–9. In time and content parallel to the Fifth Nuremberg Forum, this basic outline has been developed in a similar way in the memorandum of the Evangelical Church in Germany: *Identität und Verständigung. Standort und Perspektiven des Religionsunterrichts in der Pluralität*, Gütersloh 1994.

12. On this see J. Lähnemann, 'Nicht-christlicher Religionsunterricht – interreligiöser Unterricht' in F. Schweitzer and G. Faust-Siehl (eds), *Religion in der Grundschule. Religiöse und moralische Erziehung*, Frankfurt am Main 1994, pp.144–53.

13. Information about this can be had from Geschäftstelle de Vereins der Freunde von Neve Shalom/Wahat al Salam e.V, Sonnenrain 30, D-53757 Sankt Augustin, Germany.

14. According to H. Küng, 'Weltethos und Erziehung' in Lähnemann, *Weltethos in der Erziehung*, pp.19–34: 33f.

15. *Lehrplan für den Evangelischen Religionsunterricht an Grundschulen in Bayern*, Heilsbronn 1993, pp.10, 29ff., 57ff., 95ff.

16. Ibid, pp.13, 29, 103.

17. K.-J. Kuschel, 'Perspektiven einer Genesis-Theologie der Religionen' in Lähnemann, *Weltethos in der Erziehung*, pp.120–9.

18. G. Müller-Fahrenholz, 'Die Bedeutung der "Naturreligionen" für ein postmodernes Weltethos' in ibid., pp.95–105.

19. A variety of contributions here have grown out of the educational competition sponsored by the Global Ethic Foundation, now published in J. Lähnemann and W. Haussmann (eds), *Unterrrichtsprojekte Weltethos 1. Grundschule – Hauptschule – Sekundarstufe I. – Unterrichstprojekte Weltethos; 2. Realschule – Gymnasium – Berufsschule*, Hamburg 2000 = Pädagogische Beiträge zur Kulturbegegnung, Vols 17 and 18.

20. M. Schreiner, 'Unterrichtsmodelle gegen Rassismus/Ausländerfeindlichkeit' in Lähnemann, *Weltethos in der Erziehung*, pp.270–9.

21. H. K. Beckmann, 'Die Bedeutung religiöser Werte in der Erziehung zu Konflikt- und Friedensfähigkeit – Moglichkeiten und Grenzen' in Lähnemann, *Weltethos in der Erziehung*, pp.202–12.

22. A. T. Ariyaratne, 'Die Sarvodaya-Bewegung – Umgang mit Gandhis Prinzipien am Beispiel der ländlichen Entwicklung und interreligiösen Begegnung in Sri Lanka' in ibid., pp.334–42.

23. K. Kürzdörfer, 'Das Projekt Arche in Kiel' in ibid., pp.347–54.

24. The project is sponsored by the Deutsche Forschungsgemeinschaft and is based on the chair of Protestant Religious Education in the University of Erlangen-Nürnberg in the Faculty of Education (Prof. Lähnemann) and the chair of Religious Studies in the University of Rostock, Theological Faculty (Prof. Dr Klaus Hock). At present it covers the countries of Turkey, Iran, Egypt, Jordan and Palestine.

25. A new composite volume documents new steps in this field: J. Lähnemann (ed), *Spiritualität und ethische Erziehung – Erbe und Herausforderung der Religionen*, Hamburg 2001 = Pädagogische Beiträge zur Kulturbegegnung 20 – with 50 contributions from the main religious traditions and regions of the world.

26. R. E. Heinonen, 'Imagination und Weltverantwortung. Aus der Perspektive der Lehrerbildung' in Lähnemann, *Weltethos in der Erziehung*, pp.245–52.

27. M. Raheb, 'Konzept einer pädagogischen Zusammenarbeit von ChristInnen, MuslimInnen und JüdInnen im Nahen Osten' in ibid., pp.315–20.

28. G. Mitchell, 'Grundsätze für den Neuaufbau religiös-ethischer Erziehung in den Schulen Südafrikas' in ibid., pp.230–5.

29. G. Gebhardt, *Zum Frieden bewegen. Friedenserziehung in religiösen Friedensbewegungen. Die friedenserzieherische Tätigkeit religiöse Friedensbewegungen. Historisch-pädagogische Analyse in religionsvergleichender Typik*, Hamburg 1994 = Pädagogische Beiträge zur Kulturbegegnung 11.

DOCUMENTATION

The Autonomy of the Patient and the Muslim Patient in a Society with Pluralist Values

ILHAN ILKILIC

The question whether moral norms can be universalized independently of cultural values and religious convictions is one of the classic questions of moral philosophy. However, the controversy over this meta-ethical question is gaining special relevance in the age of globalization since the ethical relevance of decisions taken every day depends on the answer to it.

The immigration of workers into the industrial states which took place in the 1960s, the clinical research carried out by the developing countries into people in the so-called developing countries, and other reasons, have led to the encounter of doctor and patient as members of different cultures and religions becoming an everyday reality. Without doubt here a lack of knowledge about the culture and religion of the patient and the lack of a common language makes far more difficult the communication needed and consequently is also a hindrance to successful therapy or investigation.

Equally problematical, however, are the concepts in medical ethics used in a conflict of interest, since these have taken on their moral implications against the background of a particular intellectual history. Even if there is no consensus among the experts about the scope and limitations of the central principles of medical ethics – like the autonomy of patients and the duty of medical care – in everyday medicine there is a practice, in divergent forms, which follows from a particular understanding of patient autonomy or care. This becomes particularly problematical when in a conflict of interest the principles of doctor and patient as members of different cultures are understood and interpreted quite differently.

In this article I shall not venture to seek out the necessary conditions for a concept of the autonomy of the patient which has universal validity. Rather, I shall attempt to demonstrate the nature and the basic outlines of decision-making or the autonomy of the patient in Islam, one of the greatest monotheistic religions in the world, and to formulate some conclusions for medical ethics which arise from it. To do so I shall sketch out the connection between the basic Islamic sources and norms of action and the stages in Muslim decision-making. I shall also discuss the specific forms of influence of a well-established practice of religious counselling (*fatwa*) and of the third party or family on the decisions of patients.

I. The sources of Muslim norms of action

Like the word *islam*, the active participle *muslim* comes from the Arabic root *s-l-m*. The words *taslim* and *salim*, which come from the same root, mean 'be submissive' or 'be in peace'. The word *aman* (be certain/security) comes from the same root as the word *iman* (faith).[1] In the mouth of the prophet Muhammad we find the following description of *iman* (faith) and *islam*. 'Islam is based on five fundamental duties: the confession of faith – "There is no God but God, and Muhammad is God's messenger" – prayer, the legal offering, pilgrimage, and fasting during Ramadan.'[2] 'One day the prophet was in the company of some people when a man approached and asked, "What is faith?" The Prophet replied, "Faith means believing in God, his angels and in an encounter with God, in his prophets and in the resurrection."'[3]

The statements in the Muslim confession quoted do not just symbolize membership of Islam but also imply the recognition of the norms for action which result from the basic sources of Islam.[4] The structure of the statements of faith and the nature of the basic obligations are built up in such a way that in Islam the frontiers between the religious and the private in Islam are always blurred. The close connection between faith and social life ensures that faith and morality form an inseparable unity.[5] On this von Ess remarks: '1. Islam is a public religion, not a religion of interiority; 2. it seeks to have an integral grasp of human beings and the world and therefore knows no separation between the worldly and the spiritual; and 3. it sees this ideal realized in the ideal past, and therefore can understand renewal only as a return to the great and wonderful beginning . . . It is not ortho*doxy* but ortho*praxy* that is decisive: that one shows oneself to be Muslim in shared cultic practices and in shared submission to the same law.'[6]

In the early period of Islam the new Muslims came to the prophet and put a clear question to him: 'What should I do to be allowed to enter paradise?'[7] This simple question contains the elementary relationship between faith and praxis. To dwell in paradise in the other world is to be interpreted as the natural consequence of pleasing God. But gaining God's good pleasure can only happen through a practice which derives its norms of action from the main Islamic sources. These are, in order of their degrees of authority, the

Qur'an (the sacred book of Islam), the Sunna (the sayings and actions of the Prophet), the consensus of the scholars (*igma'*) and the argument from analogy (*qiyas*).[8]

In the understanding and practice of Islam, for a Muslim the Qur'an occupies the highest place among the Islamic sources. It contains the sovereign will of God and is thus guidance in earthly life for attaining the main Muslim goal of *riza-i ilahi*[9] (being well-pleasing to God). The content of its verses comprises the statements of faith (*al ahkam al-i'tiqadiya*), the basic obligations (*al-ahkam al-'amaliya*) and the moral principles *al-ahkam al-ahlaqiya*).[10] This range of content stamps all the spheres of the life of Muslims, from everyday social life to private life, and their liturgical duties. In this way the Qur'an builds a bridge between the will of God and human decisions in everyday life, by communicating the norms for a correct Muslim action. W. Montgomery Watt describes the core message of the Qur'an in the following five points: '1. God is good and omnipotent. 2. Human beings return to God to be judged on the Last Day. 3. Human beings are to show gratitude to God and worship him. 4. This is to lead human beings to deal generously with their wealth. 5. Muhammad is commanded by God to hand on this message to his fellow human beings.'[11]

Muhammad (*c*.570–632), the Prophet and proclaimer of Islam, presented the implications of the universal regulations of the Qur'an by his behaviour and gave his adherents guidance in things which were not regulated in detail by the Qur'an. 'Divine call and confession made clear once for all in him, as the Seal of the Prophets, what human nature looks like, what tasks human beings are to perform in their life, what they must hope for and fear, and how their eternal destiny will be shaped.'[12]

For a Muslim the Qur'an as divine revelation is the main source of moral good and the normative values; here the behaviour and the sayings of the Prophet Muhammad are regarded as the authentic clarification, expansion and practical concretizing of the moral content of the Qur'an. His function as lawgiver[13] in many spheres of life and his function as an interpreter[14] of the Qur'an also make the Prophet a model and an authoritative person for moral actions.[15]

II. Decision-making by the Muslim patient

Like all spheres of life, the state of sickness is one of those features of life on which Islamic faith has a special viewpoint and provides appropriate norms for action. The concept of sickness coined by the Islamic sources declares both sickness and health to be realities in life and emphasizes that health, in the sense of freedom from pain, bodily handicap or abnormalities of physique, is one of the greatest and most important gifts of God. As the Qur'an promises the sick some concessions in fundamental religious duties and through the word of God cultivates a comforting way of dealing with the sick,[16] it is difficult to conclude theologically that sickness is a direct message of the divine anger or an instrument of divine punishment. The primary Islamic sources indicate that the view that sickness is a manifestation of grace and of God's forgiveness of sins or the means of divine testing can be inferred unexceptionally from a state of sickness.[17]

Alongside these interpretations, which derive their content from the Islamic belief in the other world, on the basis of the Islamic sources and medical works discussed, two essential meanings are to be attributed to sickness, with corresponding implications for action. First, health is one of the most important gifts of God. Secondly, health is a state which is a condition for performance of the practices based on fundamental Islamic norms, i.e. the fulfilment of social and religious duties which lead the Muslim to achieve God's good pleasure.[18]

The religious conviction which declares health a good entrusted to human beings at the same time implies a human responsibility for its preservation or restoration. The understanding that human beings do not truly own their bodies but only occupy them in this world obligates them to deal with their bodies accordingly. Thus it becomes an Islamic obligation to take the necessary hygienic measures or to submit to the necessary medical procedures to preserve or restore health. For Muslims have to give an account in the world to come of their attitude to their bodies, and this is connected with reward and punishment in the world to come.

The precepts of Islamic faith not only determine the meaning attributed to sickness but also give the components of a state of sickness, like the causes of sickness, the results of investigations, methods of therapy, etc., their own significance in the decision-making process of a Muslim. The recognizable biological, chemical and physical causes of sickness are mediators of the sickness which God has created out of nothing. The Muslim regards the facts established by the medical sciences only as secondary causes and attributes these natural events to the foreknowledge of God who has inscribed every event before its appearance in the phenomenal world in the so-called primal writing. Because of this relationship, they are not mere natural events which are linked together by causal laws; rather, their manifestation is the entry of the divine custom (*sunnat Allah*) into the world of being. The concept of sickness in the Islamic sources and the interpretations of sickness which have crystallized out of the principles of faith lay down the basis for making a decision in a case of sickness. Starting from this basis, a decision by the Muslim patient contains two basic components.

The acceptance of the sickness and the attitude towards it at the level of feeling is the first phase. In this process the meaning of the illness is sought at the level of the individual Muslim world-view. The sickness is to be accepted patiently, and not in rebellion against God. Complaints about why it has happened or even accusations against God are incompatible with a Muslim disposition The patient's concrete decision crystallizes out of the second phase. The second phase, which often involves deductive conclusions from Islamic principles of morality and law, is more complex and has more levels than the first. For here not only the individual religious feeling of patients but also the way in which they interpret the norms governing action are decisive. This multiplicity of interpretations can again change, depending on the nature and severity of an illness.[19]

In general two fundamental religious preferences can be established: first, the catalogue of Islamic commandments and prohibitions the observance of which is seen as the natural implication of Islamic faith, and secondly, the preservation of the health of one's own body as a demand of God. Balancing these two preferences and interpreting them in accordance with the individual's condition often lead to the final decision by a Muslim patient on medical intervention.

Observance of the food laws and duties of prayer and the principle of freedom from bodily harm are not understood a priori to be abolished in a case of sickness, but their significance is reinterpreted. The saying of the Prophet, 'Do not allow yourself to handle what is forbidden,' clearly indicates that the food regulations or Islamic obligations apply even in a state of sickness. Conflicts which exist in practice, like refusing medication because of the Islamic food laws, confirm that this norm has a certain practical relevance. On the other hand, verses from the Qur'an clearly speak of a liberation from duties in case of sickness. The Islamic legal principle *al-darurat tubih al-mahzurat* (necessity makes the forbidden permissible), which is derived from these verses, and hadiths with a similar content, suggest another regulation of these duties in the case of sickness.

The term sickness used in the verses as a general term which does not specify the content on the one hand, and the limited medical knowledge and practices at the time of the Prophet which were carried on with his approval on the other, make it difficult for a Muslim to form a medical judgment on the basis of these two sources. New scientific and technological developments in medicine not only open up an extensive field for interpretations but also represent a challenge both for the Muslim patient affected and for the scholars who discuss these topics professionally. Thus, for example, the decisions of legal scholars on organ transplants range from strict rejection on the one hand to permission to take organs for organ transplants once brain death has been diagnosed on the other.[20]

However, the possibility of a broader spectrum of decision should not give the impression that the decision is arbitrary. Thus, for example, Islam cannot advocate refusing an operation to remove an appendix or rejecting a blood transfusion to make up for blood lost in a traffic accident, which quite certainly would save human life, since extremely high value is attached to human life. As the majority of personal decisions in medicine do not focus on these life-threatening situations, it is often not easy for the ordinary Muslim with limited theological competence to make rapid decisions in difficult cases.

III. The counselling (*fatwa*) of the Islamic legal scholar (*mufti*) and the autonomy of the patient

The Arabic word *fatwa* means counselling of a questioner (*mustafti*) by a competent scholar (*mufti*) on the basis of Islamic sources. In giving a *fatwa* the mufti uses the four acknowledged main sources of Islam already mentioned with a method which has been developed in the course of Islamic cultural history. Depending on the need, further supplementary bases of argument can be used like *istihsan* (deciding on the legitimacy), *istislah* or *ra'y* (judgment by the opinion of the individual) and also *'urf* (literally custom, or taking account of customs in coming to a verdict). The case described by the questioner will be decided on by the usual methods after specific evaluations. Depending on the decision–making process of the mufti an action can be allowed (*wagib, fard*), commendable (*mandub, sunna*), advised (*mustahabb*), allowed/approved (*mubah*), not recommended (*makruh*) or forbidden (*haram*).

The practice of giving *fatwa*s was already practised by companions of the Prophet after the Prophet's death. The systematization of the procedure and the unification of the method is attributed to as–Safi'i (died 820), the founder of a school of law, who is regarded as the father of Muslim jurisprudence. As well as the Safi'ite legal school, three legal schools which bear the names of their founders should be mentioned: Abu Hanifa (died 767), Malik ibn Anas (died 795), and Ahmad ibn Hanbal (died 855).

For a Muslim the *fatwa* serves the elementary purpose of reconstructing the norms for a practical action which exist in the Islamic sources. Formulated at an ethical level, the *fatwa* serves to give the Muslim an answer to the question 'What should I do in this situation as a Muslim?' If we transfer this question of a state of sickness, the questions can be put as follows. What role does the nature of the *fatwa* play in the decision-making of a Muslim patient? Is this influence to be seen to be a clear infringement of the self-determination of the patient, or does the *fatwa* help the Muslim patient concerned to make his or her decision in accordance with Islamic norms, which is to be regarded as a contribution to his or her well-being? How binding is the *fatwa* in respect of theological principles, and also in the practical sense? How is the verdict of the *mufti* to be regarded within the theological system? Does it make an absolute claim? May his decision with conventional methods be declared as the only one and willed by God? Tantawi, the Grand Mufti of Egypt, makes the following statements on these questions: 'I do not claim that my *fatwa* or that of the others is binding on people. Rather, I am asked and clarify the judgment in religious law, after I have striven for truth and justice and researched into the sources, in the presentation of my standpoint, and after that *whoever wishes can take over the legal view in this opinion.*'[21]

The questioner initially puts his or her question out of a private interest in a decision which according to Islamic sources is made with due competence. Without doubt the conditions required, like scholarly competence, independence, the relevant disposition, etc., contribute to the questioner's trust in the *mufti* and thus to the acceptance of his *fatwa*. However, they are not enough to make the *fatwa* directly binding on the actions of a Muslim. Not only the divergent decisions of *muftis* who belong to different schools of law but also the differences of opinion within a school of law over medical interventions show how difficult it is to unify *fatwa*s. This not surprising diversity of opinion which is to be attributed to the dynamics within Islam makes it difficult to declare a *fatwa* a sole decision willed by God and thus also something absolute.

A further crucial point for the validity of a *fatwa* in practice is the religious attitude of the patient to the *fatwa*. Questioners with religious sensibilities may not feel at ease over the action recommended in a *fatwa* and be unwilling to accept the neglect of a religious duty allowed in the *fatwa*. On such occasions in Turkish the sentence 'Here there is the side of the *fatwa* and the side of piety' is used. In some situations this implies an alternative to the decision for action suggested in the *fatwa* which derives from personal piety.[22] The lack of the necessary freedom and the lack of medical and scientific competence on the part of the *mufti*, along with the nature of the *fatwa*, which is clearly influenced by faith in technology, are obstacles to the practice indicated by the *fatwa*, which from an individual Muslim perspective can violate trust in the *fatwa* and allow its authority to be challenged.

It is striking that in the fast month of Ramadan the number of questions about *fatwa*s clearly increases. If in a case of sickness fasting risks causing damage to the body or a clear danger to life, it is clear that in the circumstances fasting is not allowed by a *fatwa*.[23] However, it often happens in Ramadan that pious Muslims with slight illnesses like headaches or back-aches do not want to make use of this permission whereby the fast could be stopped through a *fatwa*, because they do not want to lose the spiritual benefit of the fast. Such an individual decision, which can be made outside the sphere recommended in the *fatwa*, cannot, however, be regarded as a decision which goes against Islamic principles.

IV. The third party in the Muslim decision-making progress and the autonomy of the patient

The involvement of a third party or the family in a decision-making process by a patient is one of the more controversial themes within debates on the autonomy of the patient. It is not only ethically problematical if the patient is not in a position to make a competent decision, but even when a third person is involved at the wish of the patient.

There can be a variety of reasons why a patient should want the involvement of the family or a third party in a decision-making progress. A particular structure of authority in the family, the conviction in the arguments of the third party, or complete confidence in them can be some of the reasons for the acceptance of or desire for the involvement of a third party in the decision-making process. The first reason can be governed by tradition or religion, whereas the two further arguments can equally well be put forward from a secular perspective.

Responsibility for one's own decisions or actions before God and obedience to one's parents – if the parents are involved in the decision-making – are two central norms of action in the decision-making process of a Muslim patient which need more clarification here. At many points in the Qur'an responsibility for an action is attributed to the one making the decision and acting. 'Each man shall reap the fruits of his own deeds: no soul shall bear another's burden.'[24] 'No soul shall bear another's burden and each man shall be judged by his own labours; his labours shall be scrutinized and he shall be justly requited for them.'[25] 'They shall bear the full brunt of their burdens on the Day of Resurrection, together with the burdens of those who in their ignorance were misled by them (in this world).'[26] Even if the Qur'an is often referring to matters of faith when it speaks of being misled, a transference to other spheres of life where there is pressure against Islamic moral standards cannot be excluded.

The interpretation of the understanding of responsibility in a state of sickness mentioned above would then mean that Muslims bear sole responsibility before their Creator for their decisions on medical therapies and will have to give account of them in the world to come. Outside influence on a decision and action associated with it which was incompatible with the basic Islamic norms would similarly be the responsibility of the third party.

In several verses the great importance attached to obedience to parents is clear. Caring for them in old age is also an obligation laid on their children by God.[27] However, there are limits to observing their wishes and obeying them. The criterion for obedience towards parents is the acceptability of their wishes in accordance with Islamic principles of faith and norms of action. Even if these verses are focussed more on matters of faith – to repeat the argument above – they can be transferred to a case of sickness. If the religious motive clearly underlies assent to the decision of parents, two points need to be investigated. The first is whether the decision of the parents can be carried out in accordance with Islamic principles or whether for theological reasons there can be doubt. Even if there is no doubt that the decision is compatible with Islamic sources, the question has to be asked whether in this case compulsion was used.

However, it is a challenge for the doctors and the team of carers to establish the quality of family involvement, i.e. whether it is traditional or religious. Should they succeed here, how then should the significance and function of this be translated into action which can be advocated in medical ethics? How can it be decided whether traditional or religious values have more claim to acceptance in the autonomy of a patient which is to do justice to cultural values?

The possibility cannot be excluded that in the case of a cancer patient who wants to fast in his last Ramadan and therefore rejects chemotherapy parents will attempt out of compassion to deter him from this decision so that his life and his time with them is prolonged. There is often argument against this pressure in such a practical situation. But can the presence of compulsion always be clearly established? What constitutes the compulsion? If the attempts of the family to convince the patient last for two days and on the third day the patient agrees, do we speak of conviction or persuasion?

Even if the basis and quality of the assent to the family's decision cannot easily be established, even in the framework of an absolutist understanding of the autonomy of the patient it is not easy to regard this action as a clear violation of the patient's right to self-determination. For in medical ethics the justification of a decision does not depend on the random link of an action to a principle of medical ethics but rather on an intensive investigation of whether this action damages the well-being of the patient.

Conclusions

How complex the decision-making process about a medical intervention is should be evident from the foundations of the Islamic norms for action sketched out above and the influence that they have. The possibly divergent decisions of the *muftis*, even within a law school, on the one hand and the fact on the other that the character of the *fatwa* is not absolutely binding, both elements which are to be derived from the system-immanent dynamics of Islam, beyond doubt enrich the spectrum of the possible decisions to be taken with the help of a *fatwa*. The individual thought and finally the decision of the Muslim patient, depending on the particular situation and his or her religion, additionally increase the number of alternative decisions. Moreover the decision-making process is complicated by the role of a third party, the significance of which derives from the Islamic norms of action but also from the modes of action defined by tradition or custom.

Noting the many levels in Muslim self-determination helps us to assess just how difficult is the question formulated at the beginning about how far the concept of the autonomy of a patient can be universalized. Without wanting to answer this question in either the negative or the affirmative, I shall formulate two conclusions for medical ethics from this account. The first is focussed on the practice of medical ethics in a multi-cultural society where the patient is a Muslim and the doctor is not. The second relates more to the theoretical discussions on medical ethics in the Anglo-American or continental European spheres.

1. The complexity of decision-making by a Muslim which has been described here offers compelling reasons against a routine and standardized mode of procedure in the case of a conflict in medical ethics.

This conclusion is directed against two types of standardization: first the identification of the Muslim patient with the indigenous or non-Muslim patient, and secondly the automatic identification of a Muslim patient with other members of his or her religion.

2. The discussion or examination of the concept of the autonomy of the patient in relation to the question whether or not it can be universalized must not be reduced to the capacity for the reception and the integration of the religious preferences of patients into this concept.

In such discussions it is often forgotten that the patient standing outside the particular culture also has a particular concept of self-determination, even if so far it has not been worked out scientifically and there have been no philosophical reflections on it. Therefore an examination of whether particular decisions can be tolerated or integrated into the proposed concept of the autonomy of the patient cannot be regarded as proof of whether it can be universalized. Rather, a comparison between the two concepts of the autonomy of the patient should be made in accordance with their catalogue of norms and their system-immanent dynamics and modes of functioning. A precise analysis and reconstruction of the forms of providing norms in the process of decision should also be involved in this comparison, even if this requires enormous intellectual effort. The modes of procedure prove all the more important if one begins from the insight that other problems like the just distribution of resources also occur in the conflict.

Translated by John Bowden

Notes

1. Cf. T. Izutsu, *The Concept of Belief in Islamic Theology*, New York 1980, pp.57–82.
2. Buhari, *Kitab al-Iman*, no.1.
3. Ibid., no.42.
4. U. Haarmann, 'Die Pflichten des Muslim', *Saeculum* 26, 1975, pp.95ff.
5. P. Antes, *Ethik und Politik in Islam*, Stuttgart 1982, pp.40f.
6. J. von Ess, 'Islam' in E. Brunner-Traut (ed), *Die fünf grossen Weltreligionen*, Freiburg 1980, pp.70–1.
7. Cf. Tirmidi, *Kitab al-Birr*, no.2005.
8. Cf. S. Ramadan, *Das islamische Recht, Theorie und Praxis*, Marburg 1996, p.33 and A. K. Reinbart, 'Islamic Law as Islamic Ethics', *Journal of Religious Ethics* 11/2, 1983, pp.189ff.
9. This form of expression is customary in Turkish.
10. Cf. Zaidan Abd-al-Karim, *Al Madhal li-dirasat as-sari'a al-islamiya*, Beirut 1396 = 1976, p.186.
11. W. M. Watt, *Der Islam* II, Stuttgart 1985, p.82.
12. J. Bouman, *Gott und Mensch im Koran*, Darmstadt 1977, pp.206–7
13. Cf. Surah 7, 157.
14. Cf. Surah 16, 44.
15. Cf. Surah 3, 23; 3, 132; 4, 59; 4, 64; 4, 80.
16. Cf. Surah 2, 184–5; 2, 196; 4, 43; 4, 102; 5, 6; 6, 91; 24, 61; 48, 17; 73, 20.
17. Cf. I. Ilkilic, 'Bioethical Issues in the Relationship between Muslim Patient and

Non-Muslim Physician', *Biomedical Ethics. Newsletter Network for Biomedical Ethics* 5, no.3, 2000, pp.125–30.

18. It must be clear from the preceding discussion that this does not mean that only healthy people can obtain God's good pleasure.

19. Cf. I. Ilkilic, 'Das muslimische Glaubensverständnis von Tod, Gericht, Gottesgnade und deren Bedeutung für die Medizinethik', *Medizinethische Materialen* 126, Bochum 2000.

20. Cf. A. F. M. Ebrahim, *Organ Transplantation, Contemporary Islamic Legal and Ethical Perspectives,* Kuala Lumpur 1998, pp.56ff., 86ff.; M. A. Albar, *Contemporary Topics in Islamic Medicine*, Jeddah 1996, pp.7ff.; I. Ghanem, *Islamic Medical Jurisprudence*, London 1982, pp.62f.; G. I. Serour, 'Islamic Developments in Bioethics' in *Theological Developments in Bioethics, 1992–94*, Dordrecht 1997, pp.184ff.; R. Haylamaz, *Islam Huku'na göre organ ve doku nakli* (Organ Transplantation according to Islamic Law), Izmir 1993, pp.120ff., etc.

21. Quoted in B. Kraewitz, *Die Hurma: schariatrechtlicher Schutz von Eingriffen in die körperliche Unversehrtheit nach arabischen Fatwas des 20.Jahrhunderts*, Berlin dissertation 1990, p.35 (my italics).

22. Cf. F. Rahman, 'Some Key Ethical Concepts of the Qur'an', *The Journal of Religious Ethics* 11/2, Fall 1983, pp.176ff.

23. In his main work *Ihya 'ulum ad-din*, Gazali mentions some Muslims who have renounced the action of healing and belong among the 'great'. Gazali observes that it is not right to interpret this attitude as an offence against the instructions of the Prophet. Cf. Al-Gazali, *Abu Hamid Muhammad Ibn-Muhammad, Ihya' 'ulum ad-din 4*, Cairo 1352 = 1933, pp.246ff.

24. Surah 6, 164.

25. Surah 53, 39–41.

26. Surah 16, 25.

27. Cf. Surah 31, 14–15, Surah 31, 21 and Surah 17, 23–24.

DOCUMENTATION

Universal Values or a Special Ethic?
Whither Moral Theology?

DIETMAR MIETH

In the context of this issue of *Concilium* about the search for universal values it can be pointed out that Catholic moral theology is an established form of universal ethics. Its starting point is universally accessible reason (in the words of Thomas Aquinas, *secundum rationem agere*). The fact that it understands rational ethics to be at the same time an ethic of creation enables it to adopt a correlative method, namely to discover the rational grounds in belief in creation and the openness to the insights of faith in rational argumentation. The same thing is true at the level of the ethic of norms (e.g. the Ten Commandments) contained in the biblical revelation, the prophetic ethics of promise (e.g. the Sermon on the Mount) and Jesus' wisdom teaching, which seeks a link with creation ethics. The ethic of revelation also correlates with insight into the ways of the good life which are discussed in philosophy in the sense of reciprocal disclosure. Continuity with creation ethics, indeed the explicit renewal of such ethics by Jesus in the face of a special Jewish ethic, again forms a bridge to universal reason. Since on the other hand the ethic of philosophical argumentation (e.g. in Paul Ricoeur) also includes the reflective genesis and examination of convictions, the so-called ethic of faith does not remain outside universal reflection. The facts described so briefly here help Catholic moral theology usually to find rapid access to themes which need to be discussed generally, which are topical and of global relevance. Moreover, moral theology can express itself in the universal language of philosophical discourse, in which it represents a particular approach, namely the approach of a universal ethic of reason, though it does this in a non-individualistic way which preserves an adequate distance from liberal universalism. This distance is connected with a Christian view of human beings in which the person is not determined in isolation but through relationship. The result is that by its own understanding, Catholic moral theology does not set out to be either a religious or even a confessional special ethic. The organic link to the Catholic Church and the notion of

communio do not conflict with this, since in the basic model of the ethics of
Thomas Aquinas the starting point of the Catholic Church was always also
that the universalism of the solidarity of the human race corresponds to the
universality of the presence of Christ.

Presupposing all this, there is a very great danger that Catholic moral
theology is being forced by the *magisterium* of the Catholic Church along the
lines of a special ethic which rejects discussion, and that as a consequence of
this inner restriction it is also perceived from outside only as a special ethic.
This trend towards stripping Catholic moral theology of the universalism
which is mediated to it through theology and perceiving it only as the voice
of an authoritarian church structure at any rate exists in the secularistic
world, even without the 'official help' of the Catholic magisterium. Thus the
'hawks' who argue for a world without religion, a world of pluralism, toleration and freedom of conscience, and the 'hawks' of a closed church who force
any theological ideas behind the bastions of the Vatican, are in almost pre-
stabilized harmony. Outsiders like to consult the Catholic magisterium with
its Roman centralistic stamp as the authentic voice of Catholic moral theology, so that they can attack the lack of rational communicability in its
doctrine as a 'self-fulfilling prophecy'. On the other hand this magisterium
asserts the universality of moral theology only on the basis of the universality
of the presence of the Catholic Church in the world, in other words as an
omnipresence of the partial which is difficult for non-Catholic faithful to
have access to. This 'universality', which in my eyes is one-sided and in no
way corresponds to the classic expression of the tradition in Thomas
Aquinas, then at best finds a connection with inter-religious dialogue, which
replaces ethics with a procedure for ascertaining what ethical views the
religions have in common. This approach may make sense, but it must not
displace the universalistic claim of moral theology described at the beginning.

The universality thus reduced to the global presence of the church is
reinforced by the view of the central Roman magisterium that it should be
present at every point in the world church with the same authority. Here it
is asserted – and I have listened to such assertions with my own ears in some
amazement – that by means of the modern methods of communication on
the Internet, any place concerned with moral theology in any province could
reach the whole world, and that therefore Rome is more competent than
the regional episcopal magisterium, since the latter could not monitor this
global effect. Of course here an excessive estimation by the Vatican of its
own capacity for control becomes clear. At the same time the bishops are
being stripped of their power to such an extent that the more recent claims

of an intention to reform the centralism of the church seem mere rhetoric.

Moreover, there is a remarkable relationship between the responsibilities of the Congregation of Faith and the Congregation of Education in Rome, which makes the latter look like a mere post office and executive assistant in questions of theological doctrine. That has also become clear in the two most recent refusals to give a *nihil obstat* for appointments to chairs of moral theology in Germany. What is not noted here is that there are two sides to doctrine: its truth and correctness have to be examined, but it also needs to be examined to see whether it can be taught effectively, in terms of evangelization. Theological teaching must not just be measured by the checklists of the authorities on the faith; it must also be examined to see how far in given contexts and difficult areas it proclaims the faith to people in our world. Totally to do away with the fruitful tension between teaching and communication in favour of an examination of doctrine robs the Congregation of Education, which is responsible for the theological institutions, of any function.

These internal difficulties of the Catholic Church have a devastating effect not only internally but also externally. This can be made clear from a specific example, the notification by the Congregation of Faith on the moral theology of Marciano Vidal. Vidal, who also used to be director of the moral theology section of *Concilium*, is regarded by professional colleagues as an almost classic moral theologian who knows the tradition of this discipline inside out and is always concerned to do justice to the correlative method mentioned above without restricting the organic tie to the church. His movements in areas of modern challenges are always cautious and balanced. In him, after his teacher Bernhard Häring, the moral theological school of the Redemptorists has an outstanding representative, and one wonders how far with his work, which I regard as a masterly achievement of classification, a whole school or moral theology is not to be punished. For the introduction to this magisterial note by the Vatican states:

This decision does not seek to judge either the person of the author or his intention or his whole work and theological activity, but only the writings under investigation, and thus to protect the present and future well-being of the faithful, the pastors and the professors of moral theology, above all those who have been trained in the theology of the author or who recognize themselves in his statements on moral theology, so that they depart from the errors and gaps in which they have been trained or still persist, and the practical consequences of these positions in pastoral and priestly service.

Here professors of moral theology are being spoken of as immature children. The judgment relates to three books by Marciano Vidal, his handbook *Moral de actitudines*, his lexicon *Diccionario des etica teologica*, and his book *La propuesta moral de Juan Pablo II*. These books and the translations of them are 'not to be used for theological education', and the handbook is 'to be revised under the supervision of the Spanish Conference of Bishops' faith commission'. The Italian edition is especially mentioned among the translations. In addition to 'errors and ambiguities', the reason for the condemnation is the dissemination of these books and their influence on theological education. The process of examining Vidal's teaching lasted for almost two years, from December 1997 to November 1999. After that, bringing in superiors in the Redemptorist order, the Congregation sought 'to gain the explicit recognition of the existing errors and ambiguities by the author', 'to accept the verdict of the magisterium' and to be 'prepared to undertake the duty of revising the writings mentioned'.

One can imagine what underlies these sober words. One can detect even from the language how a human being is being exploited here. The declamation that neither the author nor his purpose are being incriminated is of little help, especially as a remarkable logical contradiction creeps into the passage quoted above: on the one hand the author's theology is mentioned as a whole and judged negatively, but on the other his whole work and his theological activity are not to be affected. It is stated often and not without satisfaction that Marciano Vidal has accepted the verdict and all the duties associated with it.

What is this really about? First of all the note describes in a very imprecise way the model of a 'theological ethic as autonomous morality in the Christian context' and then passes a negative judgment on it. It can clearly be recognized that the note for its part advocates a particular theological view which, while referring to statements of the magisterium, darkly intimates only one approach to moral theology. Thus it is said that 'the vertical rising dimension of Christian morality is not sufficiently emphasized' in the handbook. What is sufficiently vertical? The 'presentation of the moral content' on the basis of 'redemption, cross, grace, etc.' What has happened to Thomas's ethics of creation here, one might immediately ask. And who would ask outside the sixth commandment what has happened to redemption, cross and grace? The magisterium does not ask about the connection in the case of the seventh and eighth commandments (related to economics and the ethic of the media). Is the sphere of sexual ethics especially sacral and significant for salvation?

The diagnosis that 'on the practical level he does not accept the traditional doctrine of actions which are bad in themselves and the absolute value of norms which prohibit such actions' seems even more weighty. Now Vidal in particular has shown how ill-founded is the assertion that this doctrine as presented is simply tradition, and this doctrine is also by no means accepted in Catholic moral theology as formulated, and in its usual restriction to sexual and medical ethics.

The specific questions are related to the grey area between birth control and termination of pregnancy, sterilization, homosexuality, the objective gravity of masturbation, birth control itself, homologous insemination and the distinction between ethical and legal judgments in questions of abortion which, it is said, Vidal favours on ethical grounds.

I do not intend to go into these substantive questions here in detail, since this would presuppose an exact comparison between what the author says and how it is quoted and a critical discussion with the presuppositions on which the judgment has been made, and finally an assessment of the significance of these questions. I shall also pass over here the extensive annotations which the Congregation of Faith has supplied for its note. Here well-known passages from *Donum Veritatis* and *Splendor Veritatis* are repeated. It should be recalled once again that theology has to support the magisterium in its task of 'proclaiming the truth in the church in the last instance'. Here the talk is of 'fruitful tensions'. But the necessary 'patience for attaining maturity' which is required of theologians seems to clash with the impatience of the magisterium. The use of biblical images like 'allowing to grow' here sounds like scorn, when one know how young moral theologians are already put under pressure 'before they bud and the young shoots open', although with this image the text asserts the opposite.

So the issue here is not a matter of details but of the situation of moral theology as a theological science and as 'scientific community'. Can a magisterium which thinks and acts in this way still see moral theology at all as a science and a community for reflection? The intention to protect believers from errors has long become obsolete in a time when the faithful take their own coming of age seriously and are very interested in alternatives among the schools and approaches, and especially in a time when secular ethics is booming because it does not have an authoritarian backing and nevertheless has to face specific challenges. In such a time, which does not stop at the church's door, the faithful cannot be reached only with reasons and cannot be deterred by new spikes on old walls from accepting what seems good and right to their consciences. Particularly in this connection the reference to responsibilities, indeed to ultimate responsibility, even if it may be relevant, sounds like a flight from argumentation. The magisterium chooses a theology capable of making a contact – which, to speak quite plainly, no longer exists in the form desired as moral theology – and sours for moral theology any argumentative connection with the model of philosophical ethical discussion. Moreover here making contact by no means amounts to assimilation. Often making contact means contradicting in the name of Christian options, but this is argumentative and not declamatory contradiction.

It could happen today that a moral theologian represented a so-called Catholic position in public in secular society, that people were even ready to acknowledge his or her argument, but that they rejected the position because it came from the Catholic ghetto, from which they expect only declamations and not arguments which are open to universal insight. Credibility has gone. In this situation perhaps it would be better to send out people who recited encyclicals – but in that case the theological faculties would soon empty. The reason given for Marciano Vidal's 'errors and ambiguities' is that 'pastoral care gains the upper hand over other aspects which are fundamental to and constitutive of a complete presentation of the church's moral teaching . . .' This evaluation of the pastoral *salus animarum* is as interesting as the insistence on 'completeness' and the reduction of scholarship to 'presentation'. In these conditions scholarly moral theology is simply no longer possible: so a pastoral impetus in moral theology following Bernhard Häring is disavowed. What remains is a sterile strategy of sounding out and measuring what the advocates of truth possibly think can still be said.

Therefore regardless of how the individual views of Marciano Vidal are to be discussed – and the magisterium has not wanted to allow an opportunity for such a discussion – it means the end of moral theology as a discipline in the church if no one dares to dispute any longer because that could in some way be used in a disciplinary way against someone else. Would it not be better if the Roman magisterium were to submit what in its view were risky or even false theses first to a public theological debate, possibly also involving other theological disciplines? Would it not be better to perceive the responsibility of the central magisterium as being dialogue with the help of the 'scientific community' of moral theology? The annotation to the notification rightly points out how interesting moral theology is today to young theologians (though the reason given for this interest also refers only to processes within the church). If that is the case, people should not anxiously skirt the shifts in moral interest, which of course leave gaps. The scholarly dispute can live with gaps because these gaps can be filled in the community and no one claims to be giving a complete presentation. The scholarly process can also live with reciprocal corrections. But it cannot live with a church policy of silencing and driving out, which with its selective threatening gestures does not do justice either to the breadth of the persons involved or the ethical themes. By 'selective' I mean here not only the contingency of a relatively small body in the face of the expectation that it can examine the 'completeness' of doctrine, but also the fixation of this examination on sexual and medical ethics.

Moral theology faces perhaps the greatest test in its history. Protection does not allow any proving. The paternalistic gesture of protection for the weak in the church is today no more than a form of tutelage which no longer reaches those addressed but only serves to confirm that they have not yet come of age. Otherwise it could be that moral theology is indeed increasingly used, but Rome makes such a wrong selection from it that this discipline is no longer up to its tasks and stands helplessly when confronted with the ethical shaping of the future of the *humanum*.

Translated by John Bowden

Contributors

KARL-JOSEF KUSCHEL was born in 1948. He studied German and theology at the universities of Bochum and Tübingen. He did his doctoral studies in Tübingen, where he was an academic assistant, and from 1951 to 1995 worked at the Institute for Ecumenical Research and the Catholic Faculty there. He is now Professor of Culture and Inter-Religious Dialogue in the University of Tübingen. Among his many works are: *Jesus in der deutschsprächigen Gegenwartsliteratur* (1978); *Born Before All Time: The Dispute over Christ's Origin* (1992); *Laughter. A Theological Reflection* (1994); *Abraham: A Symbol of Hope for Jews, Christians and Muslims* (1995); *Von Streit zum Wettstreit der Religg'onen. Lessing und die Herausforderung des Islam* (1998); *The Poet as Mirror* (1999); and *Jesus im Spiegel der Weltliteratur* (1999).

Address: Sandeckerstrasse 2, D 72070 Tübingen, Germany.

DIETMAR MIETH was born in 1940 and studied theology, German and philosophy. He gained his doctorate in theology at Würzburg in 1968 and his Habilitation in theological ethics in Tübingen in 1974. He became Professor of Moral Theology in Fribourg, Switzerland, in 1974 and Professor of Theological Ethics in Tübingen in 1981. His publications include *Die Einheit von vita activa und vita contemplativa*, Regensburg 1960; *Dichtung, Glaube und Moral*, Mainz 1976; *Epik und Ethik*, Tübingen 1976; *Moral und Erfahrung*, Fribourg CH ³1983; *Meister Eckhart* (which he edited), Munich ³1986; *Gotteserfahrun – Weltverantwortung*, Munich 1982; *Die neuen Tugenden*, Düsseldorf 1984; *Geburtenregelung*, Mainz 1990; *Schwangerschaftsabbruch*, Freiburg im Breisgau 1991; *Das gläserne Glück der Liebe*, Freiburg im Breisgau 1992; *Grundbegriffe der christlichen Ethik*, Paderborn 1992 (with J. P. Wils); *Religiöse Erfahrung, Historische Modelle in christlicher Tradition*, Munich 1992, which he edited with W. Haug; and *Moraltheologie im Abseits, Antwort auf die Enzyklika 'Veritatis Splendor*, Freiburg im Breisgau ²1995, which he edited.

Address: Universität Tübingen Katholisch-Theologisches Seminar, Liebermeisterstrasse 12, 72076 Tübingen, Germany.

KONRAD RAISER is General Secretary of the World Council of Churches. A pastor, theologian and sociologist, he was born in Magdeburg in 1938. After studying theology at Tübingen, he was ordained pastor and studied sociology at Harvard. From there he went to the Protestant church of Württemberg and also worked as an industrial chaplain in Berlin and Stuttgart. As professor of thoelogy at the University of the Ruhr, he was active in the German ecumenical movement and from there went to the WCC, where he took over the reins in 1993. His main problems are tackling the financial crisis at the WCC and preventing the withdrawal of the Orthodox Churches.

Address: PO Box 2100, 1211 Geneva 2, Switzerland.

CHRISTEL HASSELMANN was born in Hanover in 1950. She is a trained teacher in an integrated school in Lower Saxony, studied religion and education for her Master's degree and in 2001 gained her PhD at the University of Hanover on 'The Way to the Global Ethic Declaration of the 1993 Parliament of the World's Religions'. She is a member of the Guidelines Commission for Teaching Values and Norms in Lower Saxony and has written scholarly articles in this area.

Address: Lärchenweg 11, D-30826 Garbsen.
E-mail: CHasselmann@t-online.de

GÜNTHER GEBHARDT was born in Straubing, Germany in 1953. He studied philosophy in Munich and Catholic theology in Paris, He gained his doctorate in Fribourg, Switzerland in 1993. Between 1984 and 1997 he was European General Secretary of the interfaith organization World Conference of the Religions for Peace (WRCP) in Geneva; in 1997–98 he was executive secretary of the Swiss Institute for Development in Biel/Bienne. Since December 1998 he has been Project Co-ordinator of the Global Ethic Foundation in Tübingen. He has written *Zum Frieden bewegen. Friedenserziehung in religiösen Friedensbewegungen*, Hamburg 1994. He has also written articles on inter-religious dialogue and peace work in the religions.

Address: Am Apfelberg 8, D 72076 Tübingen.

HILLE HAKER, who was born in 1962, is academic assistant to the chair of ethics and social ethics at the Catholic Theological Faculty of the University of Tübingen. She is a member of the interfaculty centre for ethics in the sciences, where among other things she was academic co-ordinator for the European Network for Biomedical Ethics in 1998–99. Her most important current publications cover the focal points of her work: literature and ethics (her dissertation was *Moralische Identität. Literarische Lebensgeschichten als Medium ethischer Reflexion*, Tübingen 1999) and biomedical ethics (*The Ethics of Genetics in Human Procreation*, ed. with Deryck Beyleveld, Aldershot 2000). Her Habilitationsschrift on the Ethics of Human Genetics will appear shortly.

Address: Biesingerstrasse 14, 72070 Tübingen, Germany.
E-mail: Hille.Haker@uni-tuebingen.d

FRANCIS SCHÜSSLER FIORENZA, Charles Chauncey Stillman Professor of Roman Catholic Theological Studies, began teaching at Harvard Divinity School in 1986, having taught previously at the University of Notre Dame, Villanova University, and the Catholic University of America. His primary interests are in the fields of fundamental or foundational theology, in which he explores the significance of contemporary hermeneutical theories as well as neo–pragmatic criticisms of foundationalism. His writings on political theology have sought to engage recent theories of justice, especially those of John Rawls and Jürgen Habermas, and have dealt with issues of work and welfare. He has also written on the history of nineteenth- and twentieth-century theology, focussing on both Roman Catholic and Protestant theologians. In addition to more than 100 essays in the areas of fundamental theology, hermeneutics, and political theology, his publications include the books *Foundational Theology: Jesus and the Church*; *Systematic Theology: Roman Catholic Perspectives*, edited with John Galvin; *Habermas, Modernity, and Public Theology*, edited with Don Browning; *Handbook of Catholic Theology*, edited with Wolfgang Beinart and *Modern Christian Thought Volume 2: The Twentieth Century*, written with James Livingston.

Address: Harvard University, The Divinity School, Francis Ave., Cambridge, MA 02138, USA.

HANS KÜNG was born in 1928 in Sursee, Switzerland. From 1948 to 1957 he studied philosophy and theology studies at the Gregorian University, the Sorbonne and the Institut Catholique de Paris. From 1962 to 1965 he was official theological consultant (Peritus) to the Second Vatican Council, appointed by Pope John XXIII. From 1960 to 1963 he was Professor of Fundamental Theology, and from 1963 to 1980 Professor of Dogmatic and

Ecumenical Theology at the Faculty of Catholic Theology and Director of the Institute for Ecumenical Research at the University of Tübingen; after 1980 he was Professor of Ecumenical Theology and Director of the Institute for Ecumenical Research at the University of Tübingen. In 1996 he became Professor emeritus and President of the Global Ethic Foundation. He has written many books, including *Justification*; *The Council and Reunion*; *The Church*; *Infallible?*; *On Being a Christian*; *Does God Exist?*; *Eternal Life?*; *Christianity and the World Religions*; *Theology for the Third Millennium*; *Christianity and Chinese Religion*; *Reforming the Church Today*; *Global Responsibility*; *Judaism*; *Credo*; *Great Christian Thinkers*; *Christianity*; *A Dignified Dying* (with Walter Jens); *Global Ethics for Global Politics and Economics*; *The Catholic Church. A Short History* and *Tracing the Way*: *Spiritual Dimensions of the World Religions*.

Address: Waldhäuserstrasse 23, D 72076 Tübingen.

FRIEDHELM HENGSBACH is a member of the Society of Jesus. He was born in Dortmund in 1937 and studied philosophy, theology and economics in Munich, Frankfurt and Bochum. He did his doctorate on the association of African states with the European Community. He is Professor of Christian Social Ethics at Sankt Georgen in Frankfurt am Main and Director of the Oswald von Nell Breuning Institute for Economics and Social Ethics. His publications include *Eure Armut kotzt uns an. Solidarität in der Krise*, Frankfurt 1995 and *Aus der Schieflage heraus. Demokratische Verteilung von Reichtum un Arbeit*, Bonn 1995, both with M. Möhring-Hesse and *Die andern im Blick. Christliche Gesellschaftsethik in Zeiten der Globalisierung*, Darmstadt 2001.

Address: c/o Philosophisch-Theologische Hochschule Sankt Georgen, Offenbacher Landstraße 224, 60599 Frankfurt am Main, Germany.

JOHANNES LÄHNEMANN is Professor of Religious Education at the University of Erlangen-Nuremberg. His particular focus is on education towards an encounter between religion and culture. He is a member of the Round Table of the Religions in Germany and Chairman of the Peace Education Standing Commission of the World Conference on Religion and Peace. He is the director of the research project 'The Presentation of Christianity in Schoolbooks in Islamic Countries'.

E-mail: johannes.laehnemann@ewf.uni–erlangen.de

ILHAN ILKILIC was born in 1967. He studied medicine at the University of Istanbul and Philosophy and Islamic Sciences at the Rühr University, Bochum. He is preparing his philosophical dissertation *Medizinethische Aspekte des muslimischen Krankheitsverständnisses in einer wertpluralen Gesellschaft* at the graduate college Ethik in den Wissenschaften at the University of Tübingen. Since April 2001 he has been working on the research project on human genetics and new procedures in gene- and biotechnology in the Interfaculty Centre for Ethics at the University of Tübingen.

Address: IZEW Universität Tübingen, Keplerstrasse 17, D 72074 Tübingen, Germany.

Concilium Subscription Information

Issues published in 2001

February   2001/1: *God: Experience and Mystery*
edited by Werner Jeanrond and Christoph Theobald

April   2001/2: *The Return of the Just War*
edited by María Pilar Aquino and Dietmar Mieth

June   2001/3: *The Oecumenical Constitution of Churches*
edited by Oscar Beozzo and Giuseppe Ruggieri

October   2001/4: *In Search of Universal Values*
edited by Karl-Josef Kuschel and Dietmar Mieth

December   2001/5: *Globalization and its Victims*
edited by Jon Sobrino and Felix Wilfred

New subscribers: to receive *Concilium* 2001 (five issues) anywhere in the world, please copy this form, complete it in block capitals and send it with your payment to the address below.

Please enter my subscription for Concilium 2001

☐ Individual   **£25.00**/*US$50.00*   ☐ Institutional   **£35.00**/*US$75.00*

Issues are sent by air to the USA; please add £10/US$20 for airmail dispatch to all other countries (outside Europe).

☐ I enclose a cheque payable to SCM-Canterbury Press Ltd for £/$ ....

☐ Please charge my MasterCard/Visa   Expires ....

\# ..../.............................../.............................../..............................

Signature ....

Name/Institution ....

Address ....

....

....

Telephone ....

Concilium   SCM Press   9–17 St Albans Place   London N1 0NX   England
Telephone (44) 20 7359 8033   Fax (44) 20 7359 0049
E-mail: scmpress@btinternet.com